ANSWERING LOVE'S CALL

ANSWERING LOVE'S CALL

Christian Love
and a Life of Prayer

Stephen V. Doughty

AVE MARIA PRESS
Notre Dame, IN 46556

ACKNOWLEDGMENT:

Poetry by Terry Talbot and John Michael Talbot is from the jacket of the album *The Painter*, Sparrow Records, Inc., 1980.

Library of Congress Catalog Card Number: 86-81809

International Standard Book Number: 0-87793-348-0

Cover design: Thomas Ringenberg

Cover photography: Vernon Sigl

Printed and bound in the United States of America.

for Jack and Betty Wells

Let Him paint your life
Let His Spirit be resurrected
   Upon the canvas
   Of your heart
So that Christ Himself will live
   In you
     Through you
      And with you
Then you will be a Master Painting
    Of Love.

        Terry Talbot
        John Michael Talbot

CONTENTS

1

The Call and the Struggle

You have stripped off your old behavior with your old self, and you have put on a new self which will progress towards true knowledge the more it is renewed in the image of its creator.
— Colossians 3:9-10 *(JB)*

In fact, this seems to be the rule, that every single time I want to do good it is something evil that comes to hand.
— Romans 7:21 *(JB)*

Often when I hear God's call to love, I am swiftly conscious of a struggle. This is so whether the object of my love is to be my neighbor, an older friend in need, or even a member of my family. At times the struggle can well up and grip me when I catch sight of famine-wracked bodies on the evening news, of bloated bellies, and of hollow eyes that say, "Can't you do more?" The struggle may surge forth when the phone rings at midnight and a voice on the other end tells of some sudden and desperate need. The struggle is no respecter of persons. It can arise in the face of the smallest need and the most massive of human hurts. It is a dark and brooding presence which seeks to tell me, "You can do nothing more." It urges me to turn off the news, to shut out my neighbor, or even my child. God's call says, "Love." The struggle says, "Enough. Enough."

I sense I am not alone in the struggle. We strugglers are something of an army—parents, students, clergy, religious, laity living out their faith in a tough and demanding world.

We have heard the call to love loud and clear. It first came to many of us when we were very young and some good person taught us the words of Jesus, "You shall love the Lord your God with all your heart and soul and mind, and you shall love your neighbor as yourself." The call continued as we learned the teachings to love our enemies, to sell what we have and give to the poor, to have peace among ourselves and work for reconciliation. The call hovers over lives and challenges close at hand: a lonely neighbor, an ill friend, a child or co-worker who needs our patience and our understanding. We have no trouble hearing the call to love. The call is everywhere we turn.

The struggle ensues for a variety of reasons. Fatigue can nearly overwhelm us and snuff out our capacity for love. This may happen particularly if we are engaged with a demanding work or a situation which needs our long-term devotion. Our patience may unravel. We may quite simply reach the point where we have honestly poured forth all that is within us and we need nourishment ourselves if we are to go on. "You can't pour water from an empty jug," a counselor once told a friend of mine when that friend's spirit had grown empty and dry. Sometimes we struggle to love because, practically speaking, nearly everything has gone out of us and we feel we have nothing to share.

Sometimes the struggle comes for less upright reasons than having poured forth all that is in us. I like my rest. As a matter of fact, I like it very much! And in the culture in which I find myself it is hard to refrain from padding my already well-cushioned existence with just a few more extras. Outright self-indulgence is something I can easily scoff at. Most of us in the church do. Yet the thought of a cozy withdrawal into my own little world of enjoyments is immensely appealing. Selfishness comes in many disguises. It is the old person asserting himself or herself against the new person we are to become. Sometimes boldly and sometimes with keen subtlety, selfishness struggles against the call to love.

At times the struggle arises because we honestly yearn for a greater wisdom. We wish to reach out to a bereaved neighbor, but find ourselves thinking, "I don't know what to say." We want to help a student, a child, a member of our community, but are literally at our wits' end as to what we can do. We feel extreme discomfort in the face of the world's poverty and hunger, but our discomfort is met only by a profound sense of confusion. "What, Lord, can I do? What can any of us do?" We hear love's call, and then we struggle for wisdom.

Many of us who hear love's call and then find ourselves struggling are aware of persons who have heard the call and answered well. They sensed the needs around them and gave themselves to another, to a cause, to us. Not perfectly, perhaps. Not without their times of exhaustion and wondering. Still, they loved. And in their loving they shone for us. I think of three teachers I knew while in my teenage years. Each was brilliantly gifted, both in keenness of mind and in the ability to share ideas with the young. Each could have had the pick of students to work with. Each, instead, chose to work with all, firing the interests of the quick and the slower alike. We all felt special in the eyes of these teachers. And we were. They knew how to love.

I think of a woman who gave up a successful career and all the security that went with it to work among the rural poor. That was years ago. She is still doing it. She knows how to love. I think of a man who was publicly slandered. Instead of railing back, instead of getting a lawyer for what probably would have been a successful suit, he quietly bore the hurt. Four years later, when the opportunity presented itself, he gently shared a lesson in forgiveness and integrity with the young man who had done him so much harm. He knew how to love.

I knew a member of the clergy, a short man, unassuming, soft-spoken. He was never selected for a major position in his denomination, never head of a congregation. He seldom got to enter the pulpit, there to deliver his thoughtful, quiet meditations on the scriptures. "He's not a leader," some said. "He's not quite aggressive enough for our community," commented others. Perhaps the comments were true, but as the years went by he grew to know by name every adult and every child in the immense church where he served as a perpetual assistant. In their hurt and in their joy, people turned to him. When confused, people shared with him their confusion. He listened, and he helped them toward an understanding. The man knew how to love.

We have all known such persons. Many times our acquaintance with them was brief. We spent a year in the classroom with them, a season working with them, or they entered our life at a crucial time and then, when the time passed, they were gone. Yet, though we are now physically separated, the memory of them continues to nourish us within. Other special acquaintances, of course, last far longer. Many of us can think of parents, grandparents, a special aunt or uncle or neighbor who through many years and many different situations lived out the message of love. Brief or long, our contact with such persons reminds us of a critical fact. It reminds us that at least for some people it is possible to hear love's call and answer in the way we all would like to.

For myself, though, I find I often flounder on the particulars. I suspect this is so for many. I hear love's call. I carry in my mind the fond thoughts of others who have loved well. But then it happens. A parishioner stops by with a difficult problem at 3:30 on a Friday afternoon, and do I, at the worn end of a busy week, have the patience for genuine listening? Pressures mount in my office, and do I have the sensitivity to help, right now, the associate who has suddenly asked for my aid? Someone hurts deeply another whom I love, and can I respond with something more healing, and more Christ-like, than simple anger?

Few of us ever wish to be *un*loving. That is not our aim

at all. Yet the reality we grapple with involves things which are far more complex than our personal desire to become more loving. We hear the teachings of love and vigorously nod our assent. We see the examples set by loving ones we have known, and inside we say, "That's the kind of person I want to become." But then the particulars come: the crisis, the hurt, the injustice. Our minds spin about. We wonder, "What do I do?" And if we know what to do, we may wonder, "Am I able?" In particulars, in events close at hand, we meet the struggle.

The Particulars

The particulars may well trip us up. They challenge us. They stretch us. They stand up and say, "All right now, you with your high aims, try to love *this* one!" Yet the longer I live, the more I am convinced that the particulars provide us with the greatest opportunities we have to grow more loving. Obstacles and irritations, yes, they can be that. The particulars also, though, can lead us to the channels of grace and growth we are seeking. This stands out sharply when we examine the very foundations of our faith.

First, with respect to the importance of particulars, it is clear that our Lord constantly loved through the particulars which confronted him in his daily life. A tax collector of mixed reputation scurried up a tree to get a glimpse of Jesus. Others barely noticed the man. Jesus called him down, entered his home, and blessed him. A group of women one day interrupted a serious teaching session as they pushed their children forward for a blessing. The disciples sought to send them back. Couldn't these women see that Jesus had more important things to do? Jesus rebuked the disciples, brought the children forward, and through them he taught a new lesson in love. A crowd gaped at him as he hung on the cross. Some watched in hatred, some in morbid curiosity. The pain burned in his abdomen and broke in shock waves across his back. In the midst of it all he looked at the crowd and spoke his forgiveness. This was a specific forgiveness. It arched out for the mockers, the haters, and the dully indifferent. Jesus' love was far more potent than just some generalized, all-encompassing glow. It was specific, sharp, tightly focused. It came to the particular lives and hurts and needs which gathered before him.

If we can in no way approximate the fullness of Jesus' love, we can at least learn from the direction he set. If I am buffeted by the challenges, the demands, and the occasional interruptions which burst into my life, then when I look to Jesus I am reminded that it is these very particulars which provide me with what I most need. They provide me with the opportunity to love. And if I lack the wisdom or the patience to love well in a particular situation, then that very situation provides me with the opportunity to learn. The particulars are often a challenge, but they are also an open door, a pathway, an invitation to grow.

Secondly, in addition to the example of Jesus, we find that the scriptures as a whole treat love in terms of particulars. They do this in a way which can be helpful to us. Let me share here an analogy. When I was a child, my parents introduced me to a recording of Prokofiev's delightful composition *Peter and the Wolf*. It is a piece especially suited for the young. I would play it over and over again on the ancient Victrola which had somehow survived decades of use and wound up as being my own. Gradually, like all other little children who have enjoyed this piece, I came to identify the musical themes of the various characters who inhabited this tale. Peter had a theme. The duck had a theme. So did the wolf. Once I caught on to the themes, the whole piece became that much more fun. I could cringe for the duck, hide from the wolf, urge Peter to acts of caution. I continued to experience the work as a whole, but with considerably more excitement and awareness than when I first began. The particular themes made the total work come alive.

The scriptures treat love on the broadest of scales. They do this, however, in terms of particular themes. We can grow in our comprehension of love, and of the loving life, as we become familiar with these themes. We can increase our sensitivity as we seek to hear and appropriate the particular notes of teaching sounded within these themes. Central among the themes are: *God's love for us*, the theme with which everything has begun; *our love for God*, the ongoing theme of our response; *love for our neighbors*, a theme which receives great attention and issues great demands in both the Old Testament and the New; *love for our enemies*, a difficult theme, but unmistakable in its persistence in the biblical word; *love for our community*, the theme of caring for the community of faithful persons in which we find ourselves; and the theme of *love for God's world*. A considerable amount of attention will be paid to each of these themes in the following chapters. For the moment, it is sufficient to note that when it comes to dealing with love, the scriptures too work in terms of the particular. They offer particular teachings, particular focal points for our concern and learning. We can rejoice that the scriptures sound broadly the message of love, It is, however, when we begin to deal with the particulars of this message that the message comes truly alive.

My frustration with particulars is real. The need to love in a particular situation, to act with compassion or wisdom may lie well beyond any ability I have of my own. Yet, in the midst of my frustration, I am met by two other particulars. *Jesus* in his ministry constantly loved through the particular situations which met him, no matter how difficult that might have been. This suggests that the challenges I face in my daily life, far from being hindrances to love, are the very opportunities I need. The *scriptures* in their teachings on love offer particular lines for reflection and learning. This suggests that I am at least not wholly without guidance. The struggle to answer love's call with growing swiftness and understanding is not over, but in the particulars of Jesus' love and of scriptural teaching I see the beginning of aid.

The Call and Two Gifts

In searching for aids to help us answer love's call, we find not only the particulars of Jesus' example and of scriptural teaching. These can encourage us. These can guide us in our sensitivity and understanding. They can help us as we seek to grow. Beyond this, though, we find that the call itself is accompanied by two gifts. Each of these gifts is freely given. It is important at this point that we consider both of them.

The first and most fundamental gift is that of God's Spirit working within us. This is God seeking to make us new. It is God providing wisdom when we have no wisdom at all. It is God granting patience and persistence in love when our own patience has fled and our human spirits lie exhausted. It is God acting with swiftness or gradually, however God may choose, to expand my consciousness so that I see my brother's and sister's need is truly my own. It is God living increasingly in my imperfect mind, my imperfect heart, my imperfect will.

In the final analysis, I am painfully aware that as a man who seeks to follow Jesus I shall never be able to love enough. Yet more times than I can number, the Loving One has renewed my capacity for love when of myself I could do nothing at all. In my work as a pastor, more times than I can count I have seen God create the conditions for love in situations where our human efforts toward the same end were utterly in a shambles. A loving spirit is not something that I can sit down and create. It is not something that I shall ever be able to will into existence on my own. It is, however, wholly real, and it is the free gift of the loving God.

Paul in counseling the Philippians on their own

spiritual growth writes, "It is God, for his own loving purposes, who puts both the will and the action into you." Ultimately God is the source, the great giver of love and of our loving deeds. In his letter to the Ephesians he puts it more simply still: "Glory be to him whose power, working within us, can do infinitely more than we can ask or imagine." What God can do within us lies beyond the widest scope of our thinking. Such passages as these remind us that God stands ready to build up within us what we need. In our quest to answer love's call, the first gift that meets us is the gift of the Spirit which can aid us and can work within our lives.

This leads us directly to consideration of the second gift. This gift is, quite simply, the rich tradition of spiritual disciplines which can aid us in opening to God and letting the Spirit come to work within our lives. This tradition includes the resources of contemplative and meditative prayer. It embraces such practices as imaging, sensing, feeling ourselves part of a particular scriptual scene or event. It encompasses within its broad boundaries such practices as the careful, repetitive reading of scripture passages and the offering of prayer for a special grace which the pray-er needs in his or her life.

I am a Protestant, but in the past decade of my life I have been increasingly moved by how the richness of this tradition is expressed in the *Spiritual Exercises* of Ignatius Loyola. The *Exercises* present practices which have been of immeasurable aid to devout followers of Christ for over 400 years. At the same time, I continue to be enriched by the classical insights of such writers in the Reformed Tradition as John Calvin, in his extensive work on prayer, and Matthew Henry, in his scriptural commentaries. Though their points of emphasis differed from those of St. Ignatius, the tradition they focused on and sought to extend was the same. The Wesleys in their devotional writings brought their own fresh perspective to this tradition. So too did George Fox and the

Quakers with their stress on silence and on obedience to the inner leading of God. So too did Luther in *A Simple Way to Pray*, the masterful treatise written for his barber. In modern times the tradition has found rich expression through such works as Father Henri Nouwen's *With Open Hands*, Father Thomas Green's *Opening to God*, and the Rev. Georgia Harkness' simple guide *Disciplines of the Christian Life*.

I mention the breadth of this tradition partly because it is a breadth which all of us who seek to follow Jesus need to take seriously. As his followers we are like persons sharing a common country. Naturally we are most familiar with the part of the country closest to us. We know its history, its traditions, its special treasures. Yet as we become acquainted with our neighbors across the river or over the ridge, we find an immense amount that we share in common. We find too that now and again we can extend one another's vision of what this vast realm belonging to our common Savior is really like. This is not to deny the existence of differences among us. It is not to deny the need for extended and thoughtful dialogue in many areas. At the same time, however, we are encompassed by a tradition of spirituality which is truly stunning in its dimensions. In exploring this tradition together we shall find much that unites us. We shall also find disciplines, practices, insights that can strengthen us in our efforts to show Christ's love in the world.

I mention the breadth of this tradition too because the very breadth itself attests to the vital importance of what we have been given. No portion of Christ's family is without it. In the midst of our struggles we are met by a tradition which affirms that there are ways we can become more open to the working of the Spirit. There are ways we can receive the particulars of biblical teaching and let them expand the vision of our lives. There are means by which we can focus ourselves for the renewal we need and the growth in spirit that we seek. God has given us both the wind and also the sails with which to catch the wind and use its marvelous energy. We wonder, "How can my life move in the direction of love? How can I grow more loving through all that lies ahead?" God answers, "Here is my Spirit. It can work within you. It can sustain you and lead you forth." And God answers a second time, saying to us all, "Here are my special aids. With these you can grow open to the Spirit. With these you can be stretched, made sensitive, ready to receive of the Spirit in all that you are called to do."

The Call and This Book

This book is an effort to help us answer the call to love. It seeks to provide resources which can help us grow in our responsiveness. It lifts up disciplines and patterns of prayer life which can open us to the renewing work of the Spirit. In writing the book, I have drawn heavily on my own experiences as a pastor and, even more, on those disciplines which over the years have aided me in my own struggle to grow as a follower of Jesus.

The book builds on the two fundamental points which have underlain the preceding sections of this chapter. The first of these is the plain truth that we are not perfect lovers. We are not perfect lovers of Jesus, nor are we perfect lovers of our neighbors. And at times we may not be lovers at all. In the midst of our failings and struggles, however, we encounter the second fundamental point: We are given great aid. God sends the Spirit to empower us, to sustain us, to help us grow. The very particulars which frustrate and challenge us may prove to be the places of our growth. The scriptures offer rich teaching to guide us. A broad tradition of spiritual discipline offers us ways to grow open to the Spirit, to receive of the scriptural word, to engage lovingly the world around us. To put these two fundamental points another way and bring them together: This book acknowledges the struggle and then points to the abundant sources of aid that we have.

Little more will be said of the struggle. References to it will occur in the following chapters. Doubtless, persons who work with the material they find there will make even more pertinent and helpful references to it in their own minds. From this point on, however, primary emphasis will be given to the sources of aid that we have. In presenting these I will be following a particular pattern. It may be helpful for readers of this book, retreatants, study group members to bear this pattern in mind. Each of the next six chapters focuses on a major area in which we can grow in our loving. These include such areas as our love for God, love for our neighbor, love for God's world. Within these chapters there is a set progression which includes the following elements:

The landscape — an introduction, offering an overview of the area under consideration, including challenges and opportunities for growth.

Approaches — indicating prayer suggestions and other specific aids to help us grow in this particular area.

Two exercises — offering two guided meditations on passages from scripture.

Scripture passages — suggesting further passages which persons working with this book may wish to use.

This particular progression has appeared to be the most natural way to share the resources available to us. Each chapter too will conclude with a prayer. The prayers used throughout this book are drawn from the rich variety of spiritual traditions which are available to contemporary worshipers.

In the final analysis the following pages are simply encouragers of habit, not an end in themselves. Readers will not finish the chapter on "My Love for God" and then say, "There. I've taken care of that! Now I'm ready to move on to my neighbor." Much less will anyone finish working with the book and say, "I've finally got it. I've really learned to love!" Our growth in love is both a gift of God and an ongoing process in every new situation we meet. Each year our love for God can grow. So can our love for our neighbor. So can even our love for those with whom we have had great difficulty. The process does not stop. We travel through the same areas of learning time and again in our lives. If we remain open, we can receive new understanding each time we go. The intent of this book is to encourage habits which will help us receive of God and all that God seeks to do within us as we make the journey.

2

God's Love for Us

The eternal God is your dwelling place,
and underneath are the everlasting arms.

Deuteronomy 33:27 (*RSV*)

For God so loved the world that he gave his only Son, that
whoever believes in him should not perish but have eternal
life. For God sent the Son into the world, not to condemn
the world, but that the world might be saved through him.

John 3:16-17 (*RSV*)

The Landscape

Some years ago, my wife and I had as friends a couple in their mid-30s who had adopted a girl when she was just an infant. By the time the child was a year and a half old, they would ask her, "Sarah, how big is God's love?" Sarah's arms would shoot straight away from her shoulders, her chubby fingers pointing toward the sky and the ends of the earth. An open-mouthed smile would shine all across her face. She didn't say anything when she made this response. She didn't need to.

In many other homes this might have become a rather dangerously mechanical thing. It could have been a show-off bit of piety, performed with no more feeling than, say, telling the dog to roll over. In that particular home, however, the question and answer were wholly genuine. All of us who knew how much that little girl needed her parents, and how

much they needed her, sensed the depth of feeling which underlay this play-time gesture. "How big is God's love?" The
girl's outstretched arms and her smile said it all. That love
embraces the whole creation.

The landscape of experience wherein we can meet
God's love for us is indeed vast. It includes within its bounds
not just the young and the joyful, not just that laughing girl
and her happy parents. It embraces persons at very different
stations along life's way. It encompasses the places of harshness and hurt as well as the places of joy. Let me just share
here two further incidents.

An elderly man arched his back into the pillows which
the nurse had recently adjusted on his partly raised hospital
bed. His spirits seemed good to us that afternoon. His words,
though slow, came from the same mingling of warmth and
keen intellect which we had always known. In fact, the only
noticeable change, and it had been devastatingly noticeable
during the past four days, was the ebbing of his strength. He
could see this. We all could. As he arched his back now, he
very simply gave us his word on the whole situation. "Well,
if God brings me through this, I'll be all right." He hesitated
a moment, taking his breath, and then added with what can
only be described as a deep sense of peace, "And if God
doesn't bring me through, I'll be all right then too. God will
still take care." He closed his eyes and rested. In the midst of
his pain, he had felt the assurance of God's love. Out of his
love for us, the old man wanted us to feel it too.

A further instance on the landscape of God's love concerns a friend of mine, a member of the clergy who served
for some years in an extremely difficult parish. Part of the
difficulty lay in long-standing, bitter divisions which sliced
through the parish itself. The man had gone there to heal
deep wounds, but the task was rough. "It's like a war," he
said. "If I lean so much as an inch in the direction of one
group, the other group explodes." Part of the difficulty too
lay in the immense needs of the community where the

church was located. The challenges of a changing neighbor-hood, domestic violence, and an unstable economic base weighed heavily on this good person. During the early years of his service there, he burned with the frustration of having to spend his time on the issues dividing the parish while so many obvious hurts lay in the neighborhood surrounding the church.

It is significant that after some years of this man's min-istry, the parish grew in its wholeness. Divisiveness gave way to cooperation. Groups of members began to address the needs which lay so close at hand. In light of this, perhaps even more significant is the comment the man once shared during those early, most difficult years. "At times I honestly don't know if I can continue. I just want to move somewhere else, anywhere else. When that happens, I go into the sanc-tuary. I close my eyes. I quietly say over and over again, 'O God, you are my rock and my salvation. You are my rock and my salvation.' In time, I sense the Presence. I'm able to go at it again." He had sensed the movement of God toward him in love.

As suggested by each of these incidents, the realm where we experience God's love for us is often deeply per-sonal, close at hand, intimate. We may sense that love in the voice of a friend or a parent. We may feel it as a peace that moves almost inexplicably through our hearts. We may per-ceive it working upon us to restore our perspective in the midst of a demanding situation. Though hidden from out-ward view, these movements in our inmost selves speak to us the unmistakable presence of the loving God.

Such experiences of God's love may catch hold of us at expected and familiar places. As we receive of the bread and the cup. As we sing a favorite song. As we speak to God, and then wait in silence, at a time we have set aside for years. Or that love may take us by surprise. A kind word comes to us from another, or a word of correction. We know the depth of what is being said. A sudden joy comes to us, and we feel overwhelmed by the One who has fashioned all the goodness that we know. Either way, coming through the familiar or the unexpected, the love of God is carefully aimed. It touches us deep within.

Among the most personal places where God's love meets us is in our guilt. Jesus never said lightly the words "Your sins are forgiven." He did, however, speak them often. Through the ages, all expressions of the Christian faith have continued that message. Every one of us has times of stumbling. Sometimes our stumblings are just that, a momentary falling, a wavering, a difficulty. We lose our temper or our patience or both. We slip into self-pity. We gossip, and then regret. Sometimes our stumblings are cataclysmic, for us and for the others affected by what we have done. We can never take the words of absolution lightly. We can never treat them cheaply. But among the most cleansing forms of God's love is the love that reaches toward us when we have fallen and calls us to new life again.

Beyond our own inner experiences of God's love, however, there lies a far more public backdrop. God's love here is played out not in the touching of some hidden guilt or in a sudden surge of Spirit that lifts us when we have felt utterly alone. God's love now takes form in an ancient call to wandering nomads and to the fully human crew that sprung from their line. It presents itself openly in a covenant made at Sinai with a freshly liberated people, and in laws given to awaken and guide, and again in the penetrating words of prophets. The public manifestation of God's love shines most brightly in a form born in a stable and, little more than three decades later, nailed to a cross.

The public display of God's love carries forth too in the fashioning of a people who are sent out to bring peace and healing in a troubled world. They bear with them the promise "Lo, I am with you always, even to the close of the age." This promise also is an open showing of the love.

The child who delights in the flight of a bird, or the elderly hand that cups a flower, is in intimate contact with yet another portion of God's public display of love. The human touch, the sight, the feel can grasp intuitively what the scriptures and theologians proclaim. From the very beginning, from the first incomprehensible flash in which matter was born, the Spirit has moved through creation and fashioned all things for good.

The public display of God's love shines. It meets us at all places. Yet at this very point we begin to see a primary pitfall in this whole realm of faith's experience. What we see, what we know so very well, can grow common. The familiar story can become, in moments of haste, too familiar. We may look on the backdrop of God's love, but then fail to ponder it from the depths. Even the words "You are forgiven" we can receive too quickly and too swiftly forget. The very openness of God's love lets us take it for granted. We can slide by without seeing.

Other difficulties arise on the broad landscape where God seeks to reach us with love. It is almost impossible today to write something about spirituality without adding a few vehement words against the pace of modern life. The pace, of course, deserves what it is getting. At the same time, we are growing more and more to realize that what really affects our openness to God is not the pace but rather the choices we make about it. With our daily decisions we can provide channels through which the pace washes over us. Or we can build spaces which turn the pace aside and let something richer flourish among us.

Sometimes a feeling of our own smallness can constrict our sense of God's love. "I'm not worthy." "I've done too much that was wrong." "What are we? Just little specks. We're here, and then we're gone. That's all." The expressions vary, but the effect remains the same. A cramped vision of our worth can shut out the love which seeks to reach us.

For the most part, though, we are not totally blocked by such barriers. We get caught in the rush, yes. We let good things become too familiar or we get too wrapped up in our smallness. At the same time, we worship, we pray, we read books. We seek to grow in our spirituality. We do this precisely because we sense over and over again the broad realm, both public and private, where God reaches out to us in love. And the question which presses on us is simply, "In what practical ways can we now grow more sensitive to the fullness of this love?"

Approaches

Here follow nine practices which can aid us as we seek to stay open to the fullness of God's love. These do not come as steps to be followed in sequence. Each practice has its own particular focus and each can yield its own special benefits. Readers may wish to select the one or two practices which seem most suited to their present needs and then, at a later time, take other practices under consideration.

1. The Discipline of Thanks. We so often hear that our words of thanksgiving should be spontaneous. Let them spring from the heart. Pour them forth on the moment. Let them be genuine! All this is sound advice. Yet how many times when we were children did we come away from a splendid day with a grandparent or a friend, only to hear our parents say, "Did you remember to say 'Thank you'?" We then said "Uh!" and, if we weren't too far away, we hurried back and spoke the words. As we grew older, we came to realize this business of saying "Thank you" wasn't just some flat formality. It was a chance to gather in our own hearts the joy that we had received and then pour it out. Spontaneity grew with the practice. We said "Thank you!" and then we came away with a fresher sense of all the goodness that we had been given.

In our personal prayer life, many of us need to make a discipline of giving thanks. It is so easy to get caught up in the acts of intercession and supplication. I can lose myself in the earnestness of confession or the simple joy of stillness, and then, "Ah, it's time to go." I'm out the door and haven't said a word about the blessings.

It can be helpful to set aside time each day for consciously giving thanks. During this time make an inventory of the blessings you have received. Or you may wish to focus on a particular blessing. Reflect on all the goodness that has come and on what this goodness has meant to you. Then, in quietness, offer your thanksgiving. When you do this you will be returning words that are wholly deserved. You will also be looking directly toward the One who, through all circumstances, seeks to love and aid us in our lives.

2. Journaling Our Thanks. This is a variant of the preceding practice, but an important one. In my own discipline of journaling, as in my practices of prayer, it is easy to become preoccupied with all manner of other things and forget the blessings. Here again it can be helpful to make a discipline of what is so often neglected. Write a prayer of thanks. Make a list of good gifts received. Record some refreshing moment you have seen. Such acts remind us of the love which so steadily comes our way.

3. Remembrance of Past Blessings. This spiritual exercise dates back to the writers of the Psalms who used it in times of deep personal distress (Psalms 42, 63, 143). The psalmists treasured the high points in their journey of faith. Through memory, they kept such moments present. They could recall a walk to the temple, a day of joy, a season of consolation. Through acts of deep remembering, they could be in intimate contact with those times when they had sensed God's closeness in the past. In the midst of present need, such acts of remembrance provided a fresh sense of God's steadfast love and a renewed confidence that the God who had acted to strongly in the past would act again.

We need to keep in contact with the high points on our journey of faith. Such points are not just past moments, over and done. They remain as special gifts, given for the time in which we receive them and for the future struggles we face as well. In times of need, we may recall our past blessings. And we may do this not as a means of evading present hurt. Like the psalmists, we can practice remembrance as a means of opening ourselves to the Loving One who has aided us before and who will surely aid us again.

4. Meditation on God's Public Acts of Love. Here too we have an ancient practice which reveals its early roots in the Book of Psalms. The Israelites frequently focused their thoughts on three great public acts of God's love: the creation, the deliverance from Egypt, and the giving of the law (see particularly Psalms 1, 8, 19, and 105). Steady reflection on these events nourished their sense of God's greatness. Times of vivid remembrance kindled their awe. They felt not only the immensity of what God had done; through the fullness of their meditations, they came to know that all of it had been done for them in steadfast love.

The coming of Jesus and the ongoing history of the Christian church present us with a broad range of additional focal points — Jesus' birth, his moments of teaching and healing, his passion, his resurrection, the coming of the Holy Spirit, the struggles and triumphs of the early church, the movement of the church through the ages. All these express the outreaching love of God. Each offers a fruitful place to fix our meditation.

To meditate on a particular expression of God's love, the important thing is to become present to the object of your meditation and to experience the goodness that comes through it. For this one needs both time and quietness. Select a specific focus for your meditation. If it is primarily a concept, such as the goodness of the law or the steadiness of God's love, quietly visualize places where that concept becomes real in human experience. If you meditate on an event, be present to it as a close spectator. Hear the sounds. Feel the movements. Sense the response of your own emotions.

As your meditation draws to a close, take time to give thanks for the testimony of love you have seen. Your words will be one in spirit with the psalm writer who long ago at the end of a meditation sang, "Oh Lord, our Lord, how majestic is thy name in all the earth!" (Ps 8).

5. *Meditation on God's Acts of Personal Forgiveness*. In sensing the fullness of God's love, it is helpful to meditate on the forgiveness with which God touches each of us deeply in our personal lives. There are essentially two ways we can do this. First, we can work with a passage of scripture which shows the divine mercy, such as Jesus and the woman caught in adultery or Jesus forgiving the thief on the cross. Enter the passage through meditation. Sense all that goes on between Jesus and the other. Then let Jesus turn to you. Let him speak words of mercy and of guidance directly to you. Respond to him naturally, in whatever way you feel led.

Secondly, we may wish to meditate on a specific time when God has forgiven us in the past. Again, picture the situation you were in. Sense the fullness of the unconditional love which met you there, which cleansed you and refreshed you, which helped you on your way. In either case, whether you meditate scripturally or focus on an event in your own journey of faith, close your meditation with a time of thanks for the mercy which continues to meet you.

6. *Meditation on God's Gifts to Us Now*. The living God offers us many gifts. God holds out to us the spiritual graces of love, patience, kindness, gentleness, self-control. God extends sustaining grace in our times of turmoil. God gives to each of us special talents. With calls to service and greater sensitivity, God shares with us the gift of a growing vision of what we are to do in this world.

In meditating on God's gifts to us, it is well to select one which seems of particular importance to us. Take time to reflect on the goodness of the gift. Consider the excellent things that have come through the gift and can continue to come through it. Still in meditation, turn your thoughts then to the love of the One who has freely offered the gift. You may wish to close your time of meditation with thanksgiving and with prayer to remain sensitive to the love which lies behind the gift.

7. *Focusing on God's External Kingdom.* Among the greatest signs of God's love is the kingdom. The kingdom is, of course, both "now" and "not yet." In responding to the Pharisees Jesus once said, "For you must know the kingdom of God is among you." Wherever human understanding grows, where captives are set free, where reconciliation heals ancient wounds, there shines the kingdom. It breaks forth about us in fits and starts. It comes in patches, bright patches sewn suddenly on the darker fabric of our world. Whenever this happens, the kingdom lives as a sign of God's loving will for us all. It is an image of what God calls us to become.

At the same time, the fullness of the kingdom lies beyond us. Its completeness shall come in the eternity of God. What we encounter now is only a foretaste of the everlasting wholeness that shall be. To see the kingdom which God has lovingly prepared, we must look both now and beyond.

It is certainly true that focusing thoughts on God's kingdom can become an unhealthy means of escape. This is particularly so when persons use such thoughts as a way of fleeing to something "up there," while evading their responsibilities to the kingdom right here. If, however, we keep the balance, if we vary our meditations focusing both on the places of the kingdom now and on the kingdom that is to be, the result is not at all an evasion. It is an exploration into the breadth of God's love.

8. *Affirmations of God's Caring Presence.* Affirmation entails the repetition of a special thought until that thought becomes fully a part of us. My friend who retired to the sanctuary in times of trouble and repeated over and over again, "O God, you are my rock and my salvation," was

practicing affirmation. So was a friend who, the evening before major surgery, recited to herself gently and steadily the 23rd psalm.

To use affirmations of God's caring presence, select a passage from scripture which speaks especially to you of that presence. Deuteronomy 33:27, Psalms 4:3 and 46:1-3, and John 3:16 can serve as examples. Or you may wish to write your own affirmation. We can practice affirmations nearly anywhere. The steady repetition of special words will let the meaning of those words work its way deeply into our lives.

9. Stillness in the Presence of God. As we grow in the life of prayer, we may come to a point where we no longer sense the need to speak, to ask, to pour forth our feelings. We simply wish to be still in the presence of God. We become forgetful of self. We set aside what we are and what we think we need. For a brief time we open completely to the Loving One who seeks to fill us and make us whole. Such moments leave within us deep reminders. From them we learn of the love which continues with us in the center of all things.

Practicing stillness in the presence of God is a spiritual discipline. It takes inner commitment and steady observance. I am convinced that many persons come to this quite naturally in their lives. They feel a call to times of quietness with God. They respond. And in those times of quiet they receive in ways which call them to return to the stillness again and again.

Many persons have been helped too by written guides, spiritual directors, and the long traditions of teaching on contemplative prayer. The movement in recent years toward centering prayer has been a great aid in this regard. Writings of the mystical theologians and the desert fathers continue to illuminate our understanding. So too does the Quaker practice of silence. More will be offered on this in the second of the two following exercises. For the moment it is enough to note that practicing stillness in the presence of God provides us with one of the greatest channels for opening to the fullness of God's love.

Two Exercises

The following two exercises are intended both for use in themselves and as examples of further prayer exercises which persons may develop on their own. As with the other exercises to be offered in this book, these may be used in a time of personal prayer. They may also be used in a group, with one person serving as director for the time of prayer.

Meditation on a Public Expression of God's Love
(Text: Isaiah 52:13 — 53:12)

The New Testament offers many rich passages for reflecting on the love which God showed us on the cross. In the Old Testament, the Suffering Servant passages of Isaiah provide this same focus and do so in words which often speak with freshness to our present age.

1. After a time of coming to quiet, read the entire passage slowly. Let the images it offers rise up in your mind.

2. Begin now to focus on the several great themes offered in this passage. Reflect first on the images of suffering. Call to mind the image or images which most convey to you that suffering: the disfigurement . . . or the lack of beauty . . . or the person despised and rejected . . . or the man of sorrows and acquainted with suffering . . . or the one who remains utterly silent in the midst of great pain. Take time to let this image of suffering grow in your mind.

3. Now gently move to the next theme of this passage: This suffering was for you. He bore your sufferings and carried your sorrows. He became burdened with your sins that you might be made whole. Take time to reflect on your own pains and wanderings, and see him carrying these for you.

4.   Continuing to follow the movements of the passage, focus yourself once more on the fullness of his suffering. This suffering carried him all the way to death. Look on the completeness of his self-giving, and consider the love that he has expressed for you.

5.   Because he gave himself so totally he has risen now in total victory. His sacrifice bears rich fruit, and he sees many following in his ways of wholeness. Reflect on the victory he won and on the goodness he now offers to many, and to you.

6.   Close your time of meditation offering thanks for the things that you have seen and with a simple prayer that you may keep before you the images of his love.

Stillness in the Presence of God

For the following exercise, I would suggest a duration of around 20 minutes, with the largest portion of time given to the second of its three movements.

1.   Begin with a time of quietly drawing yourself together before God. What feelings, concerns, preoccupations are you bringing to this time of prayer? What events lie ahead of you that are on your mind? Gather your feelings and thoughts together not as a means of being able to present more spoken prayers. Gather them simply as a means of being deeply in touch with yourself and of being able to come before God saying, "Here, Lord. This is how I am right now."

2.   Having gathered yourself together in silence, now gently turn your whole focus to God. Rest still in God's presence. This is not a time of listening for specific answers. It is simply a time of being fully open to the One who is wholly present to you. To aid you with your focus, you may find it helpful during this period to repeat within you a single word such as "God" or "Jesus" or "Love." Or you may find it helpful to carry a single mental image, such as light or warmth. In time

you may come to the point where, even without the aid of words or images, you receive of the One who is about you and at work within you.

3.   It is important not to break off too suddenly from such times of silent nearness. You may wish to close, therefore, with a familiar prayer that is of special meaning to you, or with thanksgiving for this time of stillness and with petition that you may be mindful of God's deep inner presence in all that lies ahead.

Persons who regularly practice stillness in the presence of God discover that God uses the stillness in a rich variety of ways. They find too that as they continue the practice they become increasingly at home in the silence and grow more sensitive to the workings of the Spirit within. If the above exercise is practiced by a group, it would be helpful for members to share the variety of their experiences afterward. If an individual wishes to practice the exercise, it would be helpful to make a commitment to do this for at least a month.

Scripture Passages

Other passages appropriate for reading and meditation:

Exodus 12:37-42

Deuteronomy 26:5-11

Psalms 8, 19, 23, 42, 51,
    63, 100, 103, 105, 116,
    131, 139:1-18, 143

Isaiah 42:1-4

Isaiah 49:1-6

Isaiah 50:4-11

Isaiah 52:13 — 53:12

Matthew 9:10-13

Mark 14:22-25

Luke 7:36-50

Luke 10:38-42

Luke 15:1-7, 8-10, 11-32

Luke 23:33-34

John 3:16-17

John 8:1-11

Romans 8:31-39

Ephesians 2:1-10

Ephesians 3:14-21

A PRAYER
To Know the Love of God

Love divine, all loves excelling,
Joy of heaven, to earth come down,
Fix in us Thy humble dwelling,
All Thy faithful mercies crown!
Jesus, Thou art all compassion,
Pure, unbounded love Thou art;
Visit us with Thy salvation,
Enter every trembling heart.

Breathe, O breathe Thy loving Spirit
Into every troubled breast!
Let us all in Thee inherit,
Let us find the promised rest.

Take away the love of sinning;
Alpha and Omega be;
End of faith, as its Beginning,
Set our hearts at liberty.

— **Charles Wesley**

3

Our Love for God

Hear, O Israel: The Lord our God is one Lord; and you shall love the Lord your God with all your heart, and with all your soul, and with all your might.
— Deuteronomy 6:4-5 (*RSV*)

The Landscape

The scene shifts now. In the preceding chapter we focused on God's movement toward us in love. Here we look on our movement toward God in return. The images of these two chapters follow in proper sequence. They fit together like the pieces of a puzzle. Out of love, God called Abraham and Sarah. Now we turn our gaze 180 degrees to those whom God has called. We see them step forth on a journey of faith which persons have followed for nearly 4,000 years. Out of love, the risen Christ showed his hands, his wounded side, and breathed the Spirit. Again we turn our gaze and we see that some, responding in love, choose to follow.

We know this same sequence in our personal lives. The pieces of the puzzle fit together the same way. We are touched by God's mercy, and if we truly comprehend the magnitude of what we have been given, our inner response is, "Lord, how can I love you more?" We hear Jesus' call to a life that is abundant and full. If we truly ponder that call, our inner self tells us, "I want to follow." We receive the gift of the bread and the cup, and if we even begin to grasp the immensity of the moment, we yearn to give of ourselves in return. On the personal level as well as on the level of God's great public acts, the landscape of our love for God is the landscape of persons responding. It is the landscape of people saying "Yes" to God, or "Here am I," or "I wish to follow and I wish to grow."

It is too, as we look on it, a landscape on which many of the most vital movements take place over time. Differing strains of Christian spirituality converge on this important point. The *Ascent of Mount Carmel* by St. John of the Cross and *Pilgrim's Progress* by John Bunyan represent what many persons rightly see as widely different approaches to the questions of spirituality and the movement of a human life toward God. The former is a pinnacle work of mystical theology. Written in the closing decades of the 16th century, it is still studied and used today. In the *Ascent*, St. John of the Cross treats in great detail the active movement of the soul toward God. He interprets the experiences which devout persons feel within. He offers counsel on how to respond to these experiences. He continues this emphasis in the *Dark Night of the Soul*, where he charts still further the progress of the soul toward the ultimate goal of union with God.

Published in 1678, *Pilgrim's Progress* receives little use today. For nearly 200 years, however, it served as a companion to the Bible in many Protestant homes. It still sounds important themes which continue at the heart of spirituality in the Reformed tradition: immersion in the active world with all the struggles, temptations and choices that this immersion entails; close attention to the guidance of scripture; a heavy emphasis on the need for God's forgiving and sustaining grace. In writing the book, Bunyan did not focus on the inward and deeply subtle journey of the soul. He offered none of the rich counsel on contemplative prayer which so abounds in the *Ascent*. Rather he gave full attention to the travels of an ordinary man named Christian as he tried, amid many fumblings, to make it out of the City of Destruction and into the Kingdom of God. Although in many ways a deeply spiritual work, *Pilgrim's Progress* can never be called mystical in the usual sense of the word. Readers don't look inward to the movement of the soul. By means of an elaborate allegory, they look to the encounters, relationships and crises of their travel through the world.

The differences between these two works are not, of course, primarily a matter of opposition. The *Ascent of Mount Carmel* and *Pilgrim's Progress* represent diverse, but complementary, explorations into how we can respond to the divine love. On the deepest level both come forth as an answer to the question "How can we, in love, return to the One who lovingly reaches out to us all?" And for our present efforts at charting the landscape where we offer that love, both works came together at this central point: Our movement toward God takes place over time. It is not instant. It is a reaching. It is a growth across the distance. For St. John of the Cross, the ascent of Mount Carmel is arduous. The sensitive and the devoted may rightly stay on one level for years before being called to the next. For John Bunyan, the pilgrimage lasted a lifetime.

We know this full well in our own lives. We have our times of deep closeness with God, and our struggles, and our wanderings. Our loving response to God does not sail forth at the moment we are confirmed and then stay fixed forever. It does not shine on the day we unite with a church, or in the hour when we offer the deepest commitment of our heart to God, and then continue to glow with that brilliance uninterrupted. The darknesses, the distractions, the times of inner testing come. Even if we do look steadily to God, even if we have sought to return our love for many years, we find, just as in any strong and true relationship, there is always more to learn. We discover new expressions of love. We learn new ways to grow more open in what we give. Our movement toward God is a movement through time.

And if the landscape of experience we look on right

now is a landscape of people responding to what God has
given, if it is a landscape on which the most important
movement takes place over time, it is also a landscape on
which we see revealed the purpose which lies at the heart of
human existence. The people who inhabit this landscape are
doing what we are all here for. They have grasped the very
center of what life is about.

Here again differing strains of spirituality converge on a
central point. Near the start of his *Spiritual Exercises* St.
Ignatius sets forth what he calls "The First Principle and
Foundation" on which the four weeks of exercises are then
built. Ignatius begins his statement of the foundation with
these words:

> God freely created us so that we might know,
> love and serve him in this life and be happy with
> him forever. God's purpose in creating us is to
> draw forth from us a response of love and service
> here on earth, so that we may attain our goal of
> everlasting happiness with him in heaven.
> (*Modern Spiritual Exercises: A Contemporary
> Reading of the Spiritual Exercises of St. Ignatius*;
> David L. Fleming, S.J., Doubleday Image, 1983,
> p. 25.)

I first heard these words some years ago while listening
to a tape and driving through the lovely ponderosa forests of
the Black Hills. My decidedly Presbyterian mindset rather
quickly wandered from the tape, the road, and back to a
question which has been shared with children in my own
religious tradition for better than 300 years. The first and
best known question of the *Westminster Shorter Catechism* is
simply:

Q. What is the chief end of man?

A. Man's chief end is to glorify God, and to enjoy him
forever.

My mind returned to the road, but I have never forgotten
that good moment.

It would be unfair to the richness of the Ignatian and the Reformed traditions to claim that they build identical structures. Quite clearly, they do not. Much of what they build, however, they build upon a single insight. Each tradition pierces to the very heart of human purpose, and there each finds the same answer. What are you and I here for? What are we to be doing? We are here to grow back toward God in love. In the ancient words, we are here to love the Lord our God with all our heart and with all our soul and with all our might.

As we take all this to the most practical of levels and look over the responses people make to God, we see persons engaged in the simplest of acts — worship, self-examination, resolution, self-offering. One person bows, another walks and reflects. Another joins with a group and sings at the top of her lungs. Another reads. Still another struggles heavily with something that has gone on inside of him for a long time. Humble acts — sometimes public and sometimes deeply private. But as we look, our varying traditions tell us that these persons share a common bond. They have found what we are here for.

The hazards in this realm of our growth are, of course, real and immediate. Idolatry has never gone out of fashion. The ancient gods have long since ceased to be a threat, but each age provides a host of new idols for people to run after, and our age is certainly no exception. Between the many definitions of what "the good life" is all about, we have more than enough idols to lead us off the track. Spiritual pride still possesses its capacity to trip us up. So too does its quieter partner, complacency. At more than one point on the path our love for God can grow misdirected, misshapen, or simply very tired. Yet the mere knowledge of this can cause us to press all the harder. We sense our need to respond to God in love. We sense it deeply. We know the pitfalls are utterly real, and so we reach out all the more to find the way.

Approaches

What specific resources do we have to help us grow in our devotion to the living God? What steady practices can give rise to more faithful movements in our minds and hearts? Our journey toward God in love is continuous, and at differing stages we will need different forms of aid. Once again the reader is encouraged to select from the following practices those few which seem most appropriate to his or her needs right now.

1. Self-Examination. Many persons engage in the discipline of self-examination on a daily basis. They set aside a regular time to review their deeds, their thoughts, their innermost feelings. Others find it helpful to engage in the practice while making a personal retreat or at two or three set times of reflection during the course of a year. Either way, persons who engage in conscious acts of self-examination are in touch with a practice which reaches back to the earliest expressions of biblical faith.

When we make a self-examination, it is well to begin with a time of coming to quiet and a prayer that God will guide us in our thoughts. We then need to probe both the positive and the negative elements in our life before God. Simple questions can aid us in each of these areas. For the positive elements: "Where have I grown closer to God? Where have my thoughts, my feelings, my specific deeds moved toward God? Where have I responded to God's call?" For the negative elements: "Where have I turned aside? Where have I ignored the call? What thoughts and feelings have I entertained, what acts have I engaged in that take me away from God?" Because self-examination is ultimately intended not for the piling up of self-congratulations, nor for the heaping up of guilt, but for our growth, it is well to end a period of self-examination with thanksgiving for the insight received and prayer to continue in the ways of positive growth.

A variant of this practice is to examine ourselves in relation to a passage of scripture or a biblical figure. Consider a parable of Jesus, or Paul's words on the qualities of the Christian life, or the faith journey of Ruth or Mary, David or Peter. Then reflect on our own faith journey. Where are we following well right now? Where are we misdirected? An exercise in this form of self-examination appears in the next section of this chapter. Whether done in direct relation to scripture, or carried out through a simple process of inner reflection, prayerful self-examination can be a major source of aid as we seek to respond more fully to God's call.

2. *Self-Offering.* Self-offering, like self-examination, can be practiced both scripturally and in a simple, reflective manner. Scripturally, you might wish to select one of the passages from the gospels where Jesus calls the disciples or summons people to walk in the ways of the kingdom. Take time to enter the passage with your imagination . . . Visualize the others who have gathered around Jesus . . . What do they look like? . . . What are they feeling? . . . Join them in looking to Jesus as he speaks . . . Begin to sense the response others make to him. How do they answer the call? . . . What do they take with them if they go? . . . And now let Jesus turn to you and invite you to follow . . . What do you sense inside? . . . How do you come forward? . . . What do you bring with you as you come? . . . What aid does Jesus give you with your hesitations? . . .

You may wish to close such a time with prayer that you continue to offer yourself freely and in loving service in all that you do.

Reflective self-offering begins with a simple act of taking stock. Consider your talents and your strengths, also your needs and weaknesses. Call to mind that place where you, and perhaps you alone, can be of service. Reflect on any persons who especially need you. Then share in prayer your talents, your strengths, your weaknesses, your opportunities, asking that you may use them all in the service of God. "Here I am, Lord, myself, just as you know me. Receive me, all that I have and all that I am, and use me according to your will." We can, of course, make such an act of self-offering in utter solitude. Many persons too find it helpful to make a reflective self-offering while coming forward to receive the sacrament of communion or while making a special act of giving in the church.

3. Reaffirmation of Our Vows. Baptism. Confirmation. Ordination. Marriage. At each of these formative moments in our life with God, vows or promises are spoken. The same holds true when we unite ourselves to a particular religious community. The same holds true for those deeply personal moments of commitment which take place between ourselves and God alone. Rightly seen, our religious vows are far more than a formality. They present the open channels along which our love for God and for God's ways can find its fullest, freest expression.

Recent decades have seen an increase in the practice of reaffirmation. On the occasion of an anniversary, couples will repeat the vows which for many years have made a sacrament of the bond between them. Various branches of the Christian church are providing formal services for the reaffirmation of pledges made at baptism, confirmation, and ordination. Laity, religious and clergy frequently use special moments in the life of the church to turn within and reaffirm the promises which they have made. Like the occasion when a vow was first pronounced, the moment of reaffirmation is far more than a simple formality. Accompanied by prayerful reflection, it can become a time when we move yet more fully into the pathways of our devotion.

4. The Discipline of Time. This is among the most obvious of spiritual disciplines, but also among the most neglected. For growth in the spirit of devotion, we need to build a daily space where we are alone with God. If we are beginning in this discipline, it is well to set aside a fixed time of half an hour and commit ourselves to hold to it for a month. We may wish to spend this time reading the scriptures or devotional material and then entering into prayer. We may spend it meditating on a passage or engaging in self-examination or having a time of stillness in the presence of God. At the end of the month we can continue the discipline of time, prayerfully engaging in those practices which appear most suited to our needs.

Even when we have followed on our spiritual journey for some years, it is still possible to let this special time slip away from us. When this happens, we need to awaken ourselves and rebuild the space once again. Our daily time with God is essential for enriching the bonds we share.

5. *Loving God Through What We Do.* As a spiritual discipline this is at least as much a matter of inner awareness as it is of outward activity. It is relatively easy to go through our round of daily business and then, after all is done, tell ourselves, "There, I've followed my calling today. I've sought to serve God in what I have done, and I hope I have done well." Certainly the hope may be a genuine one. As we moved from one activity to the next, we may well have given our best. Yet such offerings frequently come more as an afterthought than as part of the process. We act, then with varying degrees of devotion or contrition, we hope.

Loving God through what we do requires a constant inner awaremess in the midst of all our outward activity. We are taking care of a child, and inside we are asking, "Lord, help me to do this in a way that will build up your spirit of love." We are working in a store or a factory, and our inner prayer is, "Lord, make me sensitive to each need that I see today." We accept a long-term responsibility, with many decisions to make, and we don't just keep the end goal in mind. At each point along the way we seek to make decisions, conduct ourselves, encourage others in a way that will return love to the One who fashioned us.

Loving God through what we do means that in a thousand different circumstances we ask a single question: "Lord God, how can I reach back to you in love right here?" Our responses to the question are never perfect, never whole, but gradually those answers can take the love we feel within and give it expression in the busiest places of our lives.

6. *The Discipline of Steadfastness.* Virtually every significant relationship we have in life presents its periods of stress and challenge. This is surely true of our relationship with God. Most of us encounter events which we do not understand and which, perhaps for an extended period of time, we cannot square with our faith. We experience temptations to follow other ways. We pass through times of darkness.

When any of this happens we need to acknowledge openly to ourselves and to God the difficulty we are in. Repressing the problem will bring us no aid. Then we need to continue steadily in our regular paths of devotion. These can remain channels for God's grace even when it is hard for us to sense anything at all. It is helpful also to hold to assurances we have known in the past. We should bear in mind that the darkness will not last forever and that God's grace is sufficient to bear us through. The time of difficulty may not lift immediately, but if we continue steadfast in our devotion we will not be turned aside. When the harshness is over, we shall emerge wiser in our bonds with God, and more sensitive, than we were before.

7. *Sensitivity to Our Inner Yearnings.* When we feel a cold blast of air, we look about for a sweater. If we feel a dryness in the throat, without even giving the matter a second thought, we start to think where we can get a glass of water. But if we feel an emptiness in our life, or regret something we have done, where do we turn? When we experience a desire to grow spiritually, do we heed that desire or do we tuck it away for sometime later in our lives? We need to become sensitive to our inner yearnings. We need

to take inventory from time to time and then act on what we find. Our emptiness, our hopes, our desires for spiritual growth never stand by themselves. They come as signs pointing us to seek a yet closer relationship with the living God.

   8. Prayers for Growth in Our Devotion. It was in the Garden of Gethsemane that Jesus said, "The spirit is willing, but the flesh is weak." Most of us come to know full well the pertinence of those words. At times we find ourselves wishing to grow in our devotion to God, but in spite of the wishes we remain utterly stuck at a level of spirituality where all has grown too familiar. We may see a particular block in our spiritual life. Or a pattern in our thinking may turn us aside. Or an old attachment diverts us. We want the situation to pass, but it will not. Circumstances have a grip on us, and however much our spirits long for a change we cannot bring it about.

   When any of this happens, it is wholly right to seek God's aid for the devotion we ourselves cannot attain. Our prayers at this point need to be specific. Not "Lord, let me in all ways grow ever closer, ever nearer to you." Not generalized petitions, but "Lord, I feel like I'm just going through the motions right now. Help me find a way of relating to you that is fresh and free." "I'm not taking the time with you I really need to. Help me make the space." "I'm reluctant to do your will here, Lord. I'm afraid. Give me the courage." Ultimately we can focus such prayers not just on those elements which block us, but on the qualities which will aid us in our spiritual growth. Again, we should be as specific in our prayers as present insights allow. If we sense a need for greater sensitivity to God's presence, then pray for that sensitivity. If we desire wisdom in assessing the pathways we are following, then pray for that wisdom.

   We may find that we need to persist in our prayers for greater devotion. God's growth within us is often gentle and sometimes must contend with more barriers than we ourselves have initially seen. If we persist, however, God will not disappoint us. Every time we offer the prayers for greater devotion we open ourselves to the grace which can enter us, cleanse us, and redirect us from within.

Two Exercises

Self-Examination in Relation to a Scriptural Text
(Text: Colossians 3:1-17)

1. Begin with a time of quietness and a prayer to be open to the insights you need. Then read through the entire passage, noting carefully how certain characteristics of life draw us toward Christ and other characteristics lead us away.

2. Read v. 1-4. Reflect on Paul's urging that you seek the things that will carry you toward Christ.

3. Read v. 5-11. Paul lists here a broad range of negative qualities that we must shed from our lives. Which of these qualities are most troubling you right now? After listing these qualities mentally or in your journal, reflect on the harm these qualities can bring. Ask forgiveness for the times you have let these qualities rule you. Pray for God's aid in rooting them out of your life.

4. Read v. 12-17. Paul lists a variety of positive qualities that are to increase in our lives as we grow toward Christ. Reflect on the good that can come from each of these qualities. Out of this listing, select the one or two qualities which you feel you most need. Pray that you may grow in this quality, or these qualities, in your daily life.

5. Close by offering thanks for God's presence and for the insights you have received during this time of self-examination.

Growing in Touch With Inner Yearnings

Whether practiced personally or in a retreat setting, the suggested time for the following exercise is 20 to 30 minutes.

1. Take time to recall all the various feelings you have experienced in recent days. Have you known excitement? . . . hope? . . . frustration? . . . an emptiness or a sudden joy or anger? . . . humor? . . . fear? . . . other movements within? List each feeling as it comes to mind and reflect on the circumstances or setting where you experienced it.

2. Now look over your list. Each of these feelings is important, but select the one or two which seem to have been dominant.

3. Consider the one or two feelings you have selected, and reflect on each as a call to grow in your relationship with the living God. If you have been experiencing fear, in what way do you now wish to grow in your bond with God? If you have sensed an inner loneliness or deep joy, an emptiness or a time of hope, what are you reaching out for in your relationship with God? List the thoughts that come into your mind.

4. Give thanks for the inner call that comes through feelings. Pray that you may remain sensitive to your feelings and responsive to the yearnings you have right now for a closer bond with God.

Scripture Passages

Additional passages appropriate for reading and meditation:

Exodus 20:1-11
Deuteronomy 6:4-9
Joshua 24:14-24
Psalms 1:1-3, 96, 100,
    146 through 150
Isaiah 6:1-8

Luke 7:1-10
John 4:23-24
John 14:21
John 21:15-19
Romans 12:1-2
Ephesians 4:17-32

Hosea 6:6
Matthew 4:18-22
Matthew 6:1-18
Mark 9:14-29

Ephesians 5:15-20
Philippians 3:12-16
I John 4:19

A PRAYER
Self-Offering

Lord, I freely give all my freedom to you.
Take my memory, my intellect, and my entire will.
You have given me everything I am or have;
I give it all back to you to stand under your will alone.
Your love and your grace are enough for me;
I ask for nothing more.

— **St. Ignatius Loyola**

4

My Neighbor

Jesus said, "You must love the Lord your God with all your heart, with all your soul, and with all your mind. This is the greatest and the first commandment. The second resembles it: You must love your neighbor as yourself. On these two commandments hang the whole Law, and the Prophets also."

— Matthew 22:37-40 *(JB)*

Take the case, my brothers, of someone who has never done a single good act but claims he has faith. Will that faith save him? If one of the brothers or one of the sisters is in need of clothes and has not enough food to live on, and one of you says to them, "I wish you well; keep yourself warm and eat plenty," without giving them these bare necessities of life, then what good is that? Faith is like that: if good works do not go with it, it is quite dead.

— James 2:14 17 *(JB)*

The Landscape

In 1559 the Flemish master Peter Bruegel the Elder produced an engraving with the title "Charitas." As fully as any other great work of art, this engraving depicts the landscape of experience we enter when we take seriously the call to love our neighbor. In the center of the engraving stands the allegorical figure of Charity herself. With her left hand she holds a flaming heart. Her face is calm and tender. Around her cluster little knots of peasants, some hollow-faced with hunger, some crippled, some naked, some dying. The figure of Charity does not remain totally aloof from the scene. With her right hand she reaches down toward a tiny, ill-clad child who appears lost and frightened.

Viewers of this engraving soon become aware that the central figure is far from the only one responding to the needs of the crowd. In the lower right hand corner a tough old burgher throws his cloak across the back of a naked man. Others nearby join in imitating this act. In the left foreground, several persons have lugged forth enormous baskets of bread which they now pass to the hungry. Far in the distance, two persons gently lower a coffin into a pauper's grave. A man and a woman visit prisoners who have been locked in stocks. Two others carry broth into a cracked dwelling where an old man lies dying. In the middle distance several persons pour milk into the bowls of the thirsty.

The expressions on the faces of those who perform the good deeds are never syrupy, never condescending. Bruegel was no sentimentalist. At times the people who pour the milk or visit the sick look tired themselves. Some have faces etched in earnestness. A few, here and there, give off soft, genuine smiles. For the most part, though, the people simply carry on with their work. At the bottom of the engraving Bruegel has fixed a Latin motto which translates, "Expect that what is befalling others will befall you; you will be aroused to render aid only if you make your own the feelings of others who cry for help in the midst of adversity."

Bruegel's "Charitas" suggests an immense amount about the realm wherein we answer the call to love our neighbor. First, this is pre-eminently a realm of the particular and the personal. Even the figure of Charity herself can do nothing in all that sea of hurt unless she does something particular. She must enter in as personally and as particularly as those who carry broth to the sick and clothe the naked. And so it is, she reaches out her hand to a little child.

Whether the artist intended it or not, his engraving depicts the tightly limited nature of our own efforts. No one person can do it all. The man who hands over his cloak is not, at the same time, able to help the lost child. The persons who pour milk into the bowls of the thirsty are in no position to twist their heads around and talk with the prisoners behind them. Somebody else has to do that. And somebody else does, which suggests a further aspect of this realm. The realm of loving our neighbor is one of collective effort. We each have our task to do. At times we may act wholly alone, and yet we are never by ourselves. Others walk paths near our own. They ease similar hurts, or perhaps hurts which we could not ease at all. The landscape is full of people answering the call. The collective effort is stunning.

As suggested in some of Bruegel's faces, the realm of loving our neighbor is not devoid of fatigue. "How long can I keep this up?" we may ask at times, or more quietly say to ourselves, "I'm tired. I'm terribly tired." The phrase "burn out" is comtemporary. The reality has been around far longer and probably will continue long after the phrase disappears. In the landscape of loving our neighbor, fatigue is an intrusion rather than a desired element, but it is no less real for being so. And Bruegel's provocative motto points to one further element: empathy. In the area of neighbor-love, we must learn to feel. "What is he feeling right now?" "What is she sensing?" "What burdens of body and spirit do these people bear, and am I learning to carry these feelings within my own life as well?"

Beyond the elements suggested in Bruegel's "Charitas," we find that other features persistently emerge in the realm of neighbor-love. Under the influence of Christ's call, we discover that the sphere of our neighbor is an ever-expanding one. My neighbor in need is next door, across the street, or in my home. But with the passage of time, Christ teaches me that my neighbor is also the Latin American family which continues in poverty while I and my physical neighbors continue in wealth. However busy I may be with tasks close at hand, however involved in my particular calling, he teaches me that the child born under apartheid is my intimate neighbor.

The realm of neighbor-love is a realm in which Christ must challenge my preconceptions and reorder my thoughts. Does my relative comfort in some way depend on a system which takes resources from that Latin American family and millions of others like them? In the realm of neighbor-love, Christ must sometimes shatter the high walls of my indifference. Once I see the victims of apartheid as my neighbors, can I totally push them from my mind? If we follow Christ about the landscape embraced by the command to love our neighbor, we find we have embarked on an often painful and disturbing journey.

In the realm of neighbor-love, we frequently grope for understanding. Sometimes our gropings are intimate, personal, aimed at a need close by. We yearn to say or do the right thing. Sometimes our groping is vast in its scope. We come to share in the collective reaching of God's people after the pathways of obedience. "How do we use the power of Christ in relation to economic systems which perpetuate injustice or political tyrannies which shackle the lives of God's children?" "How can we advocate the rights of the oppressed without stumbling ourselves into the subtle tyrannies of paternalism and pride?" When we seek to love our neighbor, the pathways at times are anything but clear.

Ultimately, in the realm of neighbor-love, we meet God's renewing power. Amid our fatigue and our questions, amid the pains brought by empathy and by the shattering of our old thoughts, we receive the fullness of reality pointed to by Isaiah:

> Even youths shall faint and be weary,
>   and young men shall fall exhausted;
> but they who wait for the Lord
>   shall renew their strength,
>   they shall mount up with wings like eagles,
> they shall run and not be weary,
>   they shall walk and not faint (Is 40:30-31, *RSV*).

When we answer the call to love our neighbor, we are not left desolate and on our own.

The landscape wherein we are called to love our neighbor is vast. Yet early in our life of faith we learn that it is a landscape which we must enter. To sense God's love for us and to return our love to God is, by itself, never enough. It is never enough to say to our neighbor in need, "Go. Be warmed and be filled with the love of God." If we do this without meeting the practical needs, we do nothing. The love we receive from God must become incarnate in our deeds. That love must now put on our flesh and blood. It must reach out through our finite hands and our still imperfect words. If none of this happens, then the circle of God's love within us remains incomplete. God's love shall continue to work in ways far beyond our imagining, but we ourselves shall have no part in what takes place. We know that we shall not grow unless we enter the landscape. So the question again becomes, "What helps do we have?" We hear the command to love our neighbor as ourself, and then we wonder, "How may we grow in the fulfillment of this command?"

Approaches

As in the previous "Approaches" sections of this book, the following prayer suggestions are intended as an aid for us. They cannot be practiced all at once, nor are they offered here in any particular sequence. As will be indicated, some are helpful at the point of preparing us to minister to another person. Other prayer suggestions deal with such concerns as the renewal of our own spirits, growth in wisdom, and opening ourselves to God's greater vision of who our neighbors really are. Readers may wish to select those prayer aids for which they have the greatest need right now and then return to others on the list in future times of need. All of these can open us to God's aid as we move about the rich and challenging realm of neighbor-love.

1. Prayer for Openness. Before going into a situation where we are called to show love to another, it is often helpful to pause and pray for an openness within ourselves. We may wish to pray to be open and sensitive to the needs of the other. We may wish to pray for openness to the presence and leading of God within that situation.

When we seek to reach out to others in their need, we never fully know what we shall find. We can never fully guess what their response will be. A simple prayer for openness followed by a brief time of inner quiet can be the channel through which God provides the receptivity we need. "O Lord, help me sense the fullness of Jane's needs now. May I listen both with my ears and with my deepest feelings." "Loving God, make me sensitive to your presence when I'm with Tom now, and help me respond to him in the spirit of your love."

2. Prayer for God's Preparations. Many times before we pay a call or go into a specific situation of hurt, it is helpful to ask God to make preparations both within the others and within ourselves before the time of contact comes. The essence of such a prayer is utterly simple: "Lord, work within them, and work within me, so that the time we share together may be according to your will." Many persons find it helpful to visualize God as light, or as a special warmth, making those preparations both within the others and within themselves.

We never fully know what God's preparations are, nor can we dictate what they should be. Yet the prayer of preparation can open us, and those we wish to be with, to works which we never could do on our own. At the conclusion of a prayer of preparation it is often of help to pause for a brief time of stillness and then give thanks for the work of preparation which God has begun.

3. Placing in the Hands of God. When our time of being with others in their particular need is over, we may come away sensing that there is still a great deal to be done. We may feel that we have only touched the surface, even if that brief touching has seemed good and of mutual blessing. This may be an especially fitting time to offer up the entire situation for God's ongoing care. In prayer we can give thanks for the aid God gave us in our task and ask God's sustaining care now deep within the person or persons we have just seen.

4. Contemplation of the Faithful. As a source of encouragement and inner renewal, it is helpful to contemplate the lives of those who have loved well. We may wish to focus on some great and long-known figure of the faith. We may wish to focus on some good person we knew. During the time of contemplation, consider what this person sought to do. What needs did he or she seek to meet? Think on the difficulties, the discouragements, the testings this person met. Reflect on what ultimately came from this person's willingness to love a neighbor in need. When concluding, it is helpful both to give thanks for the example of the one you have thought on and to pray that you too may continue in the way of love.

A variant of this form of contemplation is to think on others who are sharing love with their neighbors right now. If we are members of an order, we may wish to focus on what others in our order are seeking to do. We may focus on members of our family. Our thoughts may turn to brothers and sisters in Christ who once were close to us and now live far away. Picture them in their work. Visualize them in their times of testing and in their ongoing acts of neighbor-love. We may conclude such a time of reflection with prayers of intercession for all those we have called to mind and with thanksgiving for the common task we share.

5. The Healing Prayer of a Friend. I have found great personal aid in this and know that many others have as well. When our own spirits are exhausted, when our own meager resources are utterly spent, we may wish to request the healing prayer of a friend. The friend can be a member of our community, a spiritual counselor, our spouse. Such a friend will often have a perspective which we ourselves lack at the moment of our need, and even if our friend has no quick response, just that friend's listening can be of aid.

We should share with our friend exactly what we feel. We need to pour out our hurt as fully as we can. We need to listen to any perspective or counsel our friend may feel led to share. Then, let our friend offer the whole situation to God in prayer. We may wish to join in the prayer ourselves. Such times of shared prayer often prove to be a wide channel for God's healing grace.

6. *Receiving of the Spirit*. Many times we simply need to be alone with God and receive the Spirit anew into our lives. We can never force a renewal which only God can give. We can, however, so turn ourselves to God's renewing power that we are open, sensitive, ready to receive.

When in need of renewal, we may find it helpful first just to come to a time of real stillness in the presence of God. We may wish to do this through the practice of breathing exercises or through the repetition of some simple prayer. After this we can share with God our emptiness, our fatigue, our need to receive of the Spirit again. We may wish to share the particulars of the situation which has left us so drained. Then, in quietness, we can picture the Spirit working within us, expanding, filling the farthest corners of our lives; or we may wish to reflect on some passage of scripture which speaks of the renewal God sends. Pray then to be sensitive to the Spirit and to receive of its power. We can close this special time with thanksgiving for God's promise of renewal in our lives.

7. *Prayer for the Purity of Our Love*. Real growth in the ability to love our neighbor involves growth in self-forgetfulness. Even the most generous-spirited of persons find it hard not to look for something in return. A smile, a "Thank you," a nod of appreciation — all these return gifts mean a lot. They are rightly a source of joy whenever they

come. Yet we must more and more learn to love as our Lord, who gave himself purely for the sake of those he came to serve. He loved us so that we might have the life we were created for. He sought nothing in return. At times we need to examine our own acts of love. We need to pray that we may love as purely and as freely as Jesus has loved us.

8. Prayer for Direction. "Sometimes I wish I were two!" I have heard that phrase from conscientious persons in all walks of life. We see more needs than we can meet. A member of the clergy may know of five persons needing deep pastoral care, yet time is available for only two. A sensitive person may see three major needs in his or her community but have the energy to address only one. A parent may feel overwhelmed by the number of family concerns which come rushing together in a single period of time. What then? Under such circumstances a simple prayer for direction can open us to God's help. Share with God the problem. Share your questions. How should you spend your time? What should you do? The answers may come in different ways. Sometimes we are led to an inner certainty and peace about the particular thing we should be doing. Sometimes we are given an opportunity to accomplish far more in a set space of time than we thought we could. We reach more lives. We are able to walk with more people in their need. The important thing, though, is that we place both the situation and our limitations in the hands of God. God then can lead us in the ways we need to go.

9. Letting God Expand Our Vision. Although our physical limitations are real, it is also true that if we would increase in the spirit of love we must grow evermore sensitive to needs in the world around us. We must let God expand our vision of who our neighbors really are. Such an expansion may happen quickly. We catch an image on television. We listen to a speaker. Suddenly a hurt which lay far from our minds seems very close and personal. We find ourselves saying, "What can I do?" Our neighborhood has grown. Sometimes the expansion is gradual. It may take place over months, or even over years, as some concern quietly mounts within our lives and presses itself upon us.

To let God expand our vision we need to cultivate certain practices and also a basic attitude. The practices should include our reading in current events or our attention to the electronic media. They should include our reading in the scriptures, particularly those passages in the prophetic works and in Jesus' teaching where attention focuses on the needy of the world. After a time of exposure to current events, rather than just hurry on to something else, it is well to pause, to reflect on the fullness of what we have just seen, and to consider any channels of response that are open to us. When the scriptures point us toward the world's needy, it is helpful to seek further insights than just the obvious one that we should reach out to the hurt and the hungry. In a time of quietness we may ask God to help us sense what these persons feel and to impress those feelings upon us. We may ask God's aid in visualizing the persons to whom we ourselves are to respond.

The basic attitude we need is a willingness to see the face of Christ in all the faces of human need, to hear his call for love in all the cries of human pain. At times the end result of prayer is not so much a coming to peace as it is a coming to earnestness about the tasks which lie before us. Such earnestness, if it is to last within our hearts, must not be of our own making. It must come as a gift, poured into us from the living God. To receive this gift we need the attitude which lets us listen for the voice of God in the midst of the world's hurts as much as we need the practices which let us know what is going on.

10. Ongoing Prayer for Wisdom. As our vision expands and time passes, our need for wisdom continues. If we are involved in a steady ministry with some particular group of persons, such as the sick or our family or our parish, we never reach the point where we can finally say, "Now I know just what to say and do." If God lifts before us the hurting of the world, as God surely will, we may soon find that not only are we looking for ways to reach out, but also we are grappling with the complex issues of economics and justice on a global scale. In any field of our endeavor answers do not come at once. We reach for wisdom all the while we seek to extend the expressions of our love.

In the realm of neighbor-love, the prayer for wisdom is an ongoing part of our lives. As in our prayers for expanded vision, it is a matter of practice and attitude. The practice involves our reading, our searching, our listening to others. It involves offering to God our uncertainties and reaching steadily after God's ways. It involves seeking to learn from each new situation we encounter. The attitude involves a willingness to pass through times of perplexity. It involves our willingness to hear God's words of counsel and correction, even when these words press us toward radical change in how we look at the world. It is an attitude of openness and expectation. If we would grow in the ways of neighbor-love, our inner prayer needs steadily to be, "Lord God, let me learn."

Two Exercises

As in the preceding "Exercises" sections of this book, the following two exercises are meant to be of use in themselves this book may wish to develop during their own times of prayer. The first exercise here focuses on the area of letting God expand our vision, the second on renewal.

An Exercise for Expanded Vision
(Text for Meditation: Matthew 25:31-46)

1. After a time of coming to quiet, read slowly the entire parable.
2. Go back, reading again v. 31-40.
    *   In quietness now call to mind images of the poor of

the world, of the naked, of the imprisoned, of the
hungry. Picture them in their places of need and in
their specific hurts.

- Take time to visualize any ways that you have
  sought to respond to their needs.
- Give thanks for the ways you have been able to
  respond, and pray that you may grow yet stronger
  in your dedication.

3. Read v. 41-46.
   - Visualize again the poor, the naked, the imprisoned,
     the hungry. Ask God to bring into your mind other
     persons, ones you have forgotten, or ignored, or
     simply have not heard of before. Hear the call of
     Christ in their call for aid.
   - Take time to consider any new or renewed efforts
     you can make at understanding and reaching out.

4. In your journal record the persons or groups of persons
   who have come into your mind. Set down the ways you
   can respond. Note any areas where you feel you need to
   grow in your sensitivity or wisdom.

5. Close with thanksgiving for the persistence of Christ's
   call. Pray for steadfastness in responding to that call.

An Exercise for Renewal
(Text for Meditation: Isaiah 40:28-31)

1. This text speaks to us of God's power to transform the
   weak and the weary. After a time of coming to quiet,
   read the verses slowly.

2. Read the verses again, this time pausing to contemplate
   the various elements lifted up in Isaiah's words:
   - God as being utterly tireless and with no weariness
     at all
   - God yearning to give strength to the weary
   - Even young ones stumbling in their fatigue
   - Persons waiting on the everlasting God to renew
     their strength

- Those persons renewed, mounting up with power, walking in the steady tasks of life and not growing faint

3. Now place yourself directly in the scene. Take time to:
   - Picture yourself in your weariness, your fatigue, your emptiness
   - Consider God yearning to fill you with new life
   - Pray that you may steadily receive of God's renewing power

4. Read the passage one last time. Give thanks to God's everpresent power and for the call to wait on that power in all your times of need.

Scripture Passages

Other passages appropriate for reading and meditation:

Leviticus 19:9-14	Luke 5:12-16
Leviticus 19:18	Luke 10:25-37
Leviticus 19:33-34	Luke 18:18-27
I Kings 19:1-8	Romans 13:9-10
Isaiah 58:1-12	I Corinthians 13:3-7
Micah 8:6-8	Philippians 2:5-11
Matthew 6:1-4	James 1:2
Matthew 22:37-39	James 2:1-9
Mark 12:28-34	James 2:14-26

A PRAYER
Lord, Make Me an Instrument

Lord, make me an instrument of your peace:
    where there is hatred, let me sow love;
    where there is injury, pardon;
    where there is doubt, faith;
    where there is despair, hope;
    where there is darkness, light;
    and where there is sadness, joy.

O Divine Master, grant that I may not so
    much seek
    to be consoled as to console,
    to be understood as to understand,
    to be loved as to love.

For it is in giving that we receive,
    it is in pardoning that we are pardoned,
    and it is in dying that we are born to
    eternal life.

                      — Attributed to St. Francis of Assisi

5

My Enemy

"If you come on your enemy's ox or donkey going astray, you must lead it back to him. If you see the donkey of a man who hates you fallen under its load, instead of keeping out of his way, go to him and help him."

— Exodus 23:4-5 (JB)

"You have heard it was said, 'You shall love your neighbor and hate your enemy.' But I say to you, Love your enemies and pray for those who persecute you, so that you may be sons of your Father who is in heaven; for he makes his sun to rise on the evil and on the good, and sends rain on the just and on the unjust. For if you love those who love you, what reward have you? Do not even the tax collectors do the same? And if you salute only your brethren, what more are you doing than others? Do not even the Gentiles do the same? You, therefore, must be perfect, as your heavenly Father is perfect."

— Matthew 5:43-48 (RSV)

The Landscape

When it comes to loving someone who has hurt me, I encounter a problem with which perhaps more than a few persons reading this chapter can identify. I am long on theory and devastatingly short on practice. From popular wisdom, from sound moral teachings, from the Bible, I know what I should do. "Hate the sin and not the sinner." "Pray for those who have hurt you." "Do not be overcome by evil, but rather overcome evil with good." The direction I need to move in is clear. But then it happens. Someone puts a dent in my fender. Or in my ego. Or in some cherished plan I have made. My anger ignites. Or far worse, someone brings deep hurt to a member of my family. Then the fires within me burn broadly. I do not know how to put them out. I may not even care to. The decision "It was unforgivable" creeps into my behavior, if not into my conscious mind. I know the "shoulds" of loving my enemy, but in seasons of crisis the practice can elude me.

The places in which we encounter the need for this special form of love are, at best, challenging. It beckons in the midst of torn relationships. It hovers over the deepest of political divisions. It speaks softly amid the slights, the nagging gestures of unfairness, and the petty complaints that drain our spirits. The need for a restoring love persists in the dull aftermath of searing injustices that nearly crush us or others we love. We can recognize clearly the call to love someone who has inflicted hurt. The trouble is, it almost invariably arises in the most difficult circumstances. At times we become utterly bewildered. Even if our intentions are the best, even if we want to love, we are left groping for just what that means.

To probe this area of our experience, and to examine its importance, I would like to share with you two persons whom I grew to know during my early years as a pastor. I change their stories here for obvious reasons, though change them only slightly. Relating the barest facts of the matter, each of these persons was a widow, each in her early 60s. In addition to losing their husbands, both women had lost a child. For both, the children's deaths had come not through a lingering illness, not through some sudden accident on the highway, but through the violent, intentional act of another human being. In short, each woman had a daughter who had been murdered while still in her late teens. Though one of the women moved more in the direction of forgiveness, I do not wish in some easy way to play them off against each other as a good example and a bad example of obedience to the teachings on love. In the immensity of their struggles, I could only have the greatest admiration for each of these persons. Taken together, I think they show both the complexity and the potential of offering love to any enemy.

The woman who could not forgive was wholly open about her feelings. "I have just never been able to do it," she said. "It wouldn't seem right if I did. If the man had harmed me directly, and I survived, then perhaps I could have forgiven. But what he did to Joyce was so totally unfair." The woman carried with her a lingering, though one would have to say understandable, bitterness over the horrible injustice that had ended so young and promising a life. Beyond this, however, she did not withdraw or turn inward. She continued to be active in her community. With what must have at first been considerable courage, she took part faithfully in the positive efforts of several volunteer charitable organizations.

As I look back after a number of years, what strikes me about this woman is not her lack of forgiveness but rather her distinct ability to avoid two other pitfalls we encounter in situations of deep hurt: denial of anger and uncontrolled rage. As persons who have been taught to forgive, Christians have a particularly strong tendency to wander into the first of these. We may want to pretend that the anger isn't there. "I'm not mad!" "I'm not hurt." We don't wish to seem unloving, even to ourselves, and so the whole cluster of turbulent feelings gets tucked away. We develop a pleasant facade. The only problem is, those feelings are still there. They are bound to break forth sometime, and when they do they can bring great harm. This woman, though, wore her feelings honestly. She owned her anger. She understood it. This, I am sure, helped her develop the perspective which let her continue many positive directions in her life.

Uncontrolled rage is a further common response to deep hurt. When it comes, it lashes out with words or even physical acts. It takes no thought for consequences. It condemns broadly and bitterly nearly all things and all persons that cross its path. If, in her hurt, my friend had so looked on life, the only proper response from those of us who had not suffered as much would have been our sympathy rather than our judgment. As it was, though, she did not respond in this way. She carried a bitterness, but it was tightly focused on one man. She bore an immense emotional scar, but she did not blame it on any of us who were her friends. She treated us, and much of life itself, with warmth. We could only admire the difficult balance she maintained. Uncontrolled rage, like denial, was not a part of her.

It was the second woman, though, who for me pushed through the outer shell of normal human experience and broke through into the realm of true forgiveness and love. "It was the most difficult thing I ever did," she told me as she described her long journey toward forgiveness. I could sense from the way she spoke the words that she meant it. She told of a deep-seated anger with which she had to contend on many occasions. She described feelings of hurt and rage which burst forth within her when she thought on the one who committed the crime. She spoke of a long period in her life when she prayed that God might cleanse her from the bitterness and help her forgive.

What had that forgiveness meant for her when it finally came? "Not a rush of warm feelings for the other person," she said. "I began to understand that the feelings were something I couldn't force." But forgiveness did mean she reached a point where she could pray genuinely for the inner healing of that other person. It meant that in her own heart she could truly speak the words of forgiveness. It meant that she went and, face to face, quietly shared the words of forgiveness with the other. "This was," she indicated, "a totally freeing experience."

What were the results of this woman's forgiveness? Was there an immediate conversion? Did there come radical change in the life of the one she forgave? We hear of such

things, but in this instance it did not happen. To all outward
appearances, the other continued to be withdrawn and
deeply hostile. "Though at least," the woman added,
"forgiveness created a greater possibility for change. This
other person no longer has my terrible anger as a barrier. I
know that in some way the love God helped me show still
beckons that person to a better way."

For the woman herself, the change was great. The
feelings of bitterness eased out of her life. With them
disappeared the sudden flashes of anger that at times had
pushed all other thoughts from her mind. In the empty
spaces left by the departure of bitterness and anger, and as a
fruit of her struggle, wholly new elements began to grow:
greater sensitivity . . . the ability to be with others in their
hurt . . . a capacity to react wisely in the midst of
stress-filled situations. As she once expressed it herself, "I
found a whole new sense of how God can help me love in
those places where I thought I couldn't love at all."

The situation faced by these two women was extreme.
All of us considering the matter surely hope that our own
capacity for loving an enemy will never be so stretched. Yet
perhaps it is the very extremity of their situation which lets
these women define for us this realm of experience. We look
to them and we are reminded that in even the lesser injuries
of our own lives, when we enter the realm of loving an
enemy we have entered a difficult place. Doing what neither
of these women did, we may stumble into patterns of denial
or uncontrolled rage. To avoid this, we need to acknowledge
our harsh feelings openly and honestly, both to ourselves and
to God. We may have to contend with these feelings for an
extended time. Ultimately, if we are to pass successfully
through this realm, we shall need the cleansing and the
guidance of the One whose love is infinitely greater than our
own. We look at all of this and we see one thing more. We
see that those who learn to love in the harshest of circumstances open up whole new pathways for the working of

love. They open pathways for those who have inflicted the hurt. These persons may or may not choose to respond, but at least the pathways are there. And those who learn to love in the harshest circumstances most certainly open up new paths of love within themselves. Their growth in love's way is strong.

Approaches

Once again readers are encouraged to select those approaches which appear most suited to their own needs. The movement toward loving persons who have harmed us is, like spiritual growth itself, a journey. In some situations one line of approach may lead us to another and to even still others before we come at last to the place of forgiveness or inner reconciliation. Over the years, and in a variety of circumstances, each of the following may be helpful to us as we seek to grow in the grace of loving those who have brought us hurt.

1. Prayer for God's Aid in Forgiving. Just as God can give us the graces of peace, wisdom or courage when we do not have them within ourselves, so too can God give us the grace of being able to forgive. If we find that we are unable to forgive, if hurt and anger continue to churn inside us and will not pass away, then often the best place for us to begin is with the prayer for God's aid in forgiving.

The prayer for God's aid in forgiving may follow any one of several helpful courses. After acknowledging our own inability to forgive and our need for God's aid, we can simply pray for a greater spirit of love within our hearts. If we are aware of a bitterness within us, we shall need to pray for the ability to set it in perspective and put it out of our lives. We may wish to recall the mercies God has shown us and then pray that we can offer that same mercy to another in return. We may wish to meditate on Jesus' forgiveness of those who brought him harm and then pray that we grow more like him in the responses we now make.

It will be wholly natural if we find times when we need to persist in praying for the ability to forgive. In response to our prayers God may reveal new emotions within us, new distresses, which we need to deal with before we approach the point of genuine forgiveness. Or we may simply need to pray long for God's aid in overcoming some particular feeling which will not go away. The lack of an instant change in our own attitude, however, need not discourage us or cause us to cease our praying. The time and the persistence involved in our prayers may be exactly what we need. Feelings of hurt can sink their roots to the absolute center of our lives. Through persistence in prayer we gradually open ourselves to the very depths and there, in the depths, God can begin the uprooting and the transformation that we seek.

2. Prayer for the Other. "I know I'm supposed to pray for the ones who have hurt me, but *what* do I pray for?" The friend who asked that question touched on a wondering which many of us may feel. We have the desire to pray for another, but when it comes to the content of our prayer we remain uncertain. Do we pray that God will bless the other person with an abundance of health and good fortune in life? These may be kind blessings to ask, but even while offering the prayer we can sense that we are missing what is really needed, both for the other and for ourselves. A few simple guidelines can help us here:

- If the person persists in actions which are destructive of self or others, then it is wholly right to pray for that person to find the blessing of a better path in life.

- If that person suffers an illness or a personal loss, this of course provides us with the occasion to pray that the person will come to know the special blessings of God's presence in the midst of his or her need.

- If the person's life appears disoriented, fractured, torn apart inside, then it is fitting to pray for that person's inner healing.

- And after honest consideration, we sometimes may find that we still do not know what to pray for. When this happens, then it is best to place the person lovingly in God's care and to ask that God will bless the person according to God's most perfect will.

Praying for someone who has hurt us is never easy. This is true not just because of our emotions, but also because of the questions we may have about just what to offer in prayer. Yet if we seek to remain sensitive to that person's situation, we can offer prayers which are wholly genuine on our part and are truly fitted to the other person's need. Such prayers not only reach out toward the other in love. They become vehicles through which God can increase our own capacity for understanding.

3. Seeking Empathy and Understanding. As a spiritual discipline, this can be of great aid in leading us to a mature love of those who have given us hurt. We should begin this practice with a time of coming to quiet and prayer for God's illumination. Then we will need to reflect carefully on the other person. What has that one been feeling? What are the pressures in his or her life? What hurts has he or she felt? Are there any ways we have been acting which have perhaps been misunderstood? We should seek to feel the other person's feelings. As closely as possible, we should come to sense the deeper needs and the emotions of this other one. We can close our time of reflection with thanksgiving for any fresh insights we have received and prayer that we may remain open to still further learnings as they come.

When we prayerfully seek to grow in empathy and understanding, we do not release the other from responsibility from what he or she has done. Nor do we release ourselves from responsibility for the ways we have responded. Rather, we reach for a heightened perspective from which we can comprehend the other person more fully, and with greater care, than we have before.

4. Counsel With Another. When we have been hurt and are having difficulty handling our feelings, it may be helpful to seek the counsel of another person. We do, of course, need to be careful about whom we call on in this regard. We should select someone who will listen well and deepen our Christian understanding, not one who will merely re-enforce our anger. A well-chosen friend may offer fresh thoughts on how we can cope with our feelings. He or she may be able to point out our own blind spots, set before us patterns in our behavior which have not been helpful, or lift up matters we need to bear in mind as we think about the one who hurt us. When we seek the counsel of another, we should not expect that person to settle everything that is churning inside us. At the same time, the insights of a friend may be just what we need to help us move in a new direction.

5. Exploring and Owning Our Feelings. "I just don't know what I feel anymore." This is a natural reaction, particularly if we have been hurt by someone close to us. We find ourselves assailed by a cluster of both negative and positive emotions. Every time we start to think one set of thoughts, a new feeling comes along and pushes us in a different direction.

When we cannot form even a basic attitude toward the one who has hurt us, it may be extremely helpful to enter into a disciplined exploration of our feelings. We need to pause, taking time to relax as fully as we can. Then let the feelings come forth within us. Resist none of them. Judge none of them. Even when they seem opposed to one another, just let them flow naturally. We should identify each feeling as it comes. Name it and write it down. When we have finished, look over the list and acknowledge that each of these feelings is our own.

This simple exercise not only helps clarify our present feelings. It lets us begin the process of sorting these feelings and determining prayerfully the direction in which we need to grow.

6. Contemplation of the Results. Frequently this can serve as a useful follow-up to the preceding exercise. "What will be the long-term results if I continue to harbor this feeling? What will be the results for the other? What will these be within me? What might be the effect on the persons around me?" We need to ask these questions too when we are considering a particular line of action. As we seek to move in the direction of love, the contemplation of results can do a great deal to help us separate the things that will upbuild from the things that will destroy.

7. Personal Contact. Personal contact with someone who has hurt us can do a great deal to serve the ways of love. For this to happen, though, we need to be wholly natural in our approach and to carry with us some purpose of reconciliation.

Being natural with someone who has hurt us is difficult. We may overcompensate by putting on a kindness that we don't really feel. We may be fearful or nervous about how we will act. To be relaxed under such circumstances may simply lie beyond our own resources. And with regard to serving the purposes of reconciliation, what should we do? Offer words of forgiveness? If so, then we need to be sure that our forgiveness is from the heart and spoken in a way that will heal. Should we apologize for our part in the difficulty? If so, then our apology will need to be offered freely, not as a gesture for which we expect something in return.

When we intend to make a healing contact, we need to offer the entire situation to God in prayer before we go. We need to ask God's aid with our nervousness or our wondering, to ask God's guidance in what we say. We need to pray for God's working within the other person and God's blessing on our coming together. We should seek the inner trust which will let us refrain from pressing for immediate results. Personal contact is a hard step, but if we take that step while drawing on God's greater love, God can create conditions for sharing which lie far beyond anything we can fashion ourselves.

8. *The Act of Good Will*. A single act of good will may do far more to build up the spirit of love than many words. This insight goes all the way back to the book of Exodus with its down-to-earth instructions on helping an enemy whose beast is stumbling under its load. St. Paul shared the same truth when he quoted the Book of Proverbs to the Christians at Rome: " 'If your enemy is hungry, feed him; if he is thirsty, give him drink; for by so doing you will heap burning coals upon his head.' Do not be overcome by evil, but overcome evil with good." A gesture of genuine kindness can break down the barriers, melt the cold feelings. A visit to the hospital, meal brought in at a time of crisis — the actions will vary according to the need, but if we watch carefully we will each see places where we can initiate a healing gesture of good will.

9. *When Reconciliation Is Not Accepted*. In some situations we reach a point where we have done all that we honestly can and the other still does not respond. The person remains hostile, withdrawn, or wrapped up in ways that we do not understand. To all outward appearances he or she barely notices the offerings of love. We may sense that further direct efforts on our part will only result in added rejection or perhaps even increase the person's negative behavior. This is a deeply painful situation, but still not one which lies beyond the realm of a loving, caring response on our part.

When all efforts at reconciliation have been rejected, the most loving thing we can do is commit that other person to God's care and then seek God's cleansing from any lingering bitterness in our own life. Ask that God work within that person for wholeness, knowing as we ask this that God's inner work is often hidden and takes place over time. Pray that the person will have God's abiding care. Then we need to ask that God will help us set aside any hurtful feelings that are still our own. We may need to continue in this pattern of prayer for some time. This is wholly natural. We are moving into a new way of expressing our love. Yet in the situations of greatest difficulty, surely the most loving and freeing response we can make is to place the other person, and ourselves, in God's ongoing care.

Two Exercises

Seeking Empathy and Understanding

1. Begin with a time of recollecting a situation in which you were hurt. Do this not as a means of drawing up old feelings and bringing them forth again, but as a means of growing in touch with the full circumstances of what happened. Call to mind the one who brought the hurt, and pray for God's illumination in understanding that person.

2. Reflect thoughtfully now on the other person. Are there any special hurts or pressures this one may have been feeling? Any long-term needs or deprivations of spirit? Any habitual fears? Consider too your own actions. Is there anything you did which might have been misunderstood? Done with greater sensitivity? Not done at all? . . . Or perhaps you needed to act just as you did. It is helpful to know that too.

3. Insofar as you can, take time now to experience the other person's emotions . . . any frustrations . . . any fears . . . any inner hurts. Feeling these does not mean that you accept them as being justified on the other person's part, but it does mean that you are coming to a deeper sense of how that person has been reacting within.

4.   Write down any new insight you have received. Give
     thanks for any fresh understanding, praying that you
     may act wisely in light of it and will remain open to
     further insights as they come.

Exploring and Owning Our Feelings

1.   Select a situation in which you have truly mixed
     feelings about the person who gave you hurt. Then,
     still as a beginning to the exercise, take time to relax as
     fully as you can.

2.   Turn your thoughts directly to the one who hurt you.
     Let the feelings come forth. As a feeling comes and
     develops, give it a name and write it down. Anger, fear,
     dread, sympathy, or whatever it may be. Some feelings
     may linger for a time. Let the process continue until
     you sense that, at least for the present, all feelings have
     risen to the surface.

3.   Look over the list of your feelings. Take time to reflect
     on each of them and how right now each is a part of
     you.

4.   In prayer acknowledge to God the cluster of feelings
     you are carrying within. Ask that you may continue to
     be sensitive to all of them and may begin the process of
     sorting them and dealing with them according to God's
     will.

As we develop clarity on our feelings toward the person
who hurt us, still other emotions may surface. New insights
will come on which feelings we need to nourish and which
ones we need to let go. In particularly intense situations, it
will be helpful to repeat this exercise on a weekly or
biweekly basis until we come to the point where our feelings
are truly resolved.

Scripture Passages

Passages appropriate for study and meditation:

Genesis 4:1-16	Matthew 18:21-35
Genesis 50:15-21	Luke 6:27-36
Exodus 20:13	Luke 23:32-38
Proverbs 25:21-22	Acts 7:54 — 8:1
I Samuel 24:1-19	Romans 12:14-20
Matthew 5:7	I Corinthians 4:11-13
Matthew 5:21-26	Ephesians 4:26-27
Matthew 6:9-15	James 1:19-20
Matthew 7:1-5	I Peter 3:8-17

A PRAYER
To Show Christ's Mercy

Thou hast the true and perfect gentleness,
No harshness hast Thou and no bitterness:
O grant us the grace we find in Thee,
That we may dwell in perfect unity.

—**John Calvin**

6

My Community

"I give you a new commandment:
love one another;
just as I have loved you,
you also must love one another.
By this love you have for one another
everyone will know that you are my disciples."

— John 13:34-35 *(JB)*

If we live by the truth and in love, we shall grow in all ways
into Christ, who is the head by whom the whole body is fit-
ted and joined together, every joint adding its own strength,
for each separate part to work according to its function. So
the body grows until it has built itself up, in love.

— Ephesians 4:15-16 *(JB)*

The Landscape

"There are times when living in community absolutely
exasperates the life out of me," said the old man. He issued a
huge puff of air from under his mustache. "But," he
continued, "it is also where I most grow." His was the only
head of white hair in the room. The rest were blond, black,
one redhead. Some were men, some women. None of the
men in the group showed even the first hints of getting bald.
They were all young, full of hope, and they had gathered to
hear him talk about the 30 years he had lived as a member
of a religious community. The force with which he said
"absolutely exasperates the life out of me" startled them.
They hadn't expected it. But the twinkle in his eyes when he

said, "It is also where I most grow," kept them listening. They wanted to know more.

If that marvelous old man's opening statement did not immediately portray all the subtleties of community life, his words at least conveyed something of its scope! Exasperation . . . growth. I am convinced that if we omit either of these elements from our understanding, we will never fully grasp what Christian community life entails. The exasperations we may wish to deny, to exclude from any picture we paint, to pretend they aren't there at all. The old man who spoke that night was too wise to do this. He knew better. Whatever form of Christian community life we relate to, the exasperations break in at least from time to time. In little ways and in big, they can get to us. "If I have to listen to Sam go on and on and on just one more time, I think I will go out of my mind." "If Gloria would only be a little less self-righteous, I think I might find some inner peace." "If only our group would stop its squabblings, we might actually get something done for somebody else."

As for the growth, we may at first perceive it more by implication than by direct experience. The growth is quiet, like a seed planted in a field or a bush growing by a stream. Only when we look back over time do we exclaim with gratitude, "See what has happened!" Yet for all the quietness with which the growth in Christian community may take place, any reading of the New Testament lets us know that the fashioning of community was a major concern of our Lord. He did not just call persons to his own side. He called them to be with one another. He counseled them in the ways of love, and it was as a body that he sent them out to do his works. It has been this way from the very start: Christian community is meant to stretch us. It is at once the school where we learn love's ways and the vehicle through which we can more effectively share love's light with the world around. Whatever the personal difficulties we encounter, whatever the exasperations, we sense that Christian community is a realm we must enter if we are to mature in the ways of love.

The forms which Christian community can take vary greatly. If I were to name from my own life's experience those communities which have nourished and stretched me, surely the six small congregations I now pastor would be among them. So would each of the churches I have served in the past. No two of these have ever been alike. Each has disclosed its own character, its own strengths, its own weaknesses, its own unique opportunities for service and growth. Like human beings gifted with different personalities, however, all of them have shared the same basic call. Each in its own particular way has carried the potential to nourish the growth of love within me, within its members, and within the world which surrounds it. The same, I am sure, holds true throughout the entire family of Christ's people. For many of us, the parish in which we live is where we meet both the richness and the challenge of Christian community.

As my mind presses further along the line of life's experience, I encounter other forms of Christian community which have touched me and offered their nourishment. I recall three formal religious orders. One, Carmelite, maintained a monastery near where I attended college. One, Reformed in its origins, reaches out from the community of Taize in France with a compelling call to Christian unity. One, Jesuit, carries on the work of spiritual renewal at a retreat house six hours from where I live. With quiet counsel each of these communities has in some special way ministered to me. I recall too the community which formed among students and faculty where I attended seminary. The community struggled, differed, fought at times, groped after its identity, but it also unquestionably took shape and gave life.

When we look out over the realm that encompasses Christian community, we find no single mold from which all communities are cast. Dotting the entire landscape we see parishes. We also see monastic groups. We glimpse clusters of families which, in the city and the country, have drawn together to live in common life. Here and there we spot Bible study groups, support groups, groups of persons united in ministry to a particular hurt.

Even the outward behavior of these groups differs. Some are solemn, reserved, formal in their worship and their deliberations. Others jump and shout. Some speak in tongues. Some sit in silence and wait on the presence of God. In some gatherings nearly every member carries a crucifix. In others they all keep close a particular translation of the Bible. Different forms. Different approaches. Different expressions. And yet as we scan the landscape, we realize that over even the tiniest assembly there hangs the promise, "Where two or three come together in my name, there I am in the midst of them." At least potentially. At least if people open themselves in community, something truly special can happen.

It is this "something truly special" which causes persons to press further into the realm of community. It is important at the outset to note that community is the scene of both testing and growth. It is important to note the rich variety of community forms. But then there was the matter of the twinkle in that old man's eyes. What was he sensing and trying to convey? What does community offer to those who truly enter in? What do we encounter at the center of it?

At the center of Christian community we encounter the living Christ. It is Christ whom we meet there and it is from him that we then grow. To express the matter this way is, of course, to engage in something of an abstraction. It is to state the idea without reaching beyond it for the concrete experience. We need to move more in the direction of specifics. In what ways does the meeting take place? At what points does the encounter come? No listing of specifics will fully exhaust the possibilities, yet even a basic overview of the territory catches the richness of what can happen.

The moment of mutual support is surely among the central points at which participants in Christian community encounter the living Christ. From the beginning we have been called to be a people who laugh with those who laugh, who weep unashamedly with those who weep, and who listen, watch, wait with one another in our need. Such support extends not only to our high points and our hurts. Consciously borne in mind, it undergirds the pathways we walk in the world. Even when we are apart, we know we are not alone. We have brothers and sisters who walk similar paths, face similar struggles, and carry us in prayer even as we carry them. In such mutual support, the living Christ is at work among us and the ways of his love increase.

Christ seeks to move among us too at the points of mutual responsibility. In even a small community, different persons bear differing gifts. Wherever this is so, we share responsibility not merely to accept or tolerate the differences. We certainly are not to take one another's gifts for granted. Rather we each carry the responsibility to appreciate actively one another's gifts, to provide encouragement, and to strive to have our gifts flow together in ways which will strengthen the entire community. When divisions slice through community life, or even petty differences, we share responsibility to work things out. We are not to bury the matter, but to talk. We are not to avoid, but to deal face to face. We each are to care for one another's growth. "Will what I am about to do help my sister . . . my brother . . . or will it hurt? Will it encourage, or will it only confuse?" In Christian community we are responsible not just to Christ, but also for one another. Wherever we attend to our mutual responsibilities, we encounter the upbuilding work of our Lord.

We also meet the living Christ through the witness which a community makes in the world. In any faithful Christian community, Christ becomes present through a reaching out beyond the community. One group may extend itself through a ministry of prayer and teaching. Another may encourage its members in a variety of services. Another will seek to aid a particular gathering of neighbors. Still other groups may give themselves to the cause of nuclear disarmament, or justice for political prisoners, or the provision of health care for the utterly destitute. The points of reaching out will vary as widely as the needs which cover the earth. Yet wherever a Christian community touches the world with love, the living Christ is present. He is at work.

We all know how swiftly each of these blessings can be set aside. By its own choice a community can turn in upon itself. Individual members may grow indifferent to the life they share together, insensitive to what really can happen among them. They may take the community for granted, participating out of habit and nothing more. They may treat the inevitable irritations as excuses to drift off rather than as opportunities for growth in understanding. They simply may cease to participate at all. Whole communities too can bloat with pride, go flat with self-generated boredom, or choke on their own internal politics. These things we know only too well. We hardly need to be reminded. We have seen them happen. Through our participation, many of us have felt the pain.

The old man who spoke that night had obviously felt some of the pain. He didn't try to hide it from his young listeners. But for him the pain and the exasperation were simply one reality within a far larger and ultimately triumphant reality. What mattered most to him were not the moments of obvious failure and tension. What mattered most, and gave him such childlike joy, was the stunning reality of Christ present in a body of people, teaching them how to love and helping them show that love to the world.

Approaches

Approaches to the upbuilding of Christian community vary greatly. Some focus on opening the community to the work of the Spirit and to the instructions found in scripture. Some foster the practices of appreciation and mutual support. Some offer ways to deal with tensions in community life. Each of these approaches is needed. Eight main approaches follow here.

1. The Habit of Intercession. Few spiritual disciplines can so open a community to the upbuilding work of the Spirit as the habit of intercession. Few disciplines can serve as so broad a channel for the working of God's grace in community life. Lengthy works have appeared on the subject of intercessory prayer. Doubtless they shall continue to. There shall never arise any single way to cover all the insights and all the honest questions which surround this subject. It is perhaps sufficient here to note that the best of these writings all point to the simple fact that the riches of intercession become most clearly understood not through theorizing but through steady practice of the discipline itself. We enter in, and bit by bit we grow to understand.

When practiced in its fullness, intercession is both communal and individual. In its times of gathering for worship, the community as a whole needs to pray regularly for those members who are of special concern. Some communities will, on a rotating basis, offer all members by name whether they are near or working in some distant place. It is wholly fitting too for communities to make regular intercession for their own unity, their special efforts at mission and engagement in the world, their continued spiritual growth. Within the parishes I have served, I have sometimes known smaller groups which kept a steady discipline of intercession for the worship life of the congregation, for Bible study groups, for youth events, for a deepening of the spirit of unity and love among us all. For an entire community, the intercessions of a body of persons within it can provide a special channel for God's grace.

In acts of individual intercession, the practices of visualization and thoughtful reflection can enrich the experience of prayer and deepen the sensitivity with which we offer our prayer. Take time at the start to picture the person or situation which is the object of our prayer. Consider quietly all the good that is there, all the strengths. Then focus on the specific need: the illness, the weakness, the division, or the challenge, the opportunity for growth and service. After letting our mind rest clearly on the object of concern we can make our intercession for God's aid, lifting all the particulars we have called forth within. As we conclude the time of prayer, it is well to visualize or reflect on God working for wholeness in the situation, to give thanks for the gift of intercession, and to pray that we remain open to the variety of ways in which God may answer our prayer.

In the context of community life, as in all other contexts, intercessory prayer is an ongoing process. It is, in essence, dialogue with God. We do not present God with our demands, our dictations, our rock-solid opinions of what must happen next. Rather we offer up the deepest yearnings of our love for one another and then wait, openly, on the loving God's response. As new directions emerge, we continue in the dialogue. When practiced in this fashion, intercessory prayer renders us and the whole community more receptive to God's loving, unifying care.

2. The Practice of Appreciation. It is so easy to take one another for granted! Bob is a sensitive listener. Tom administers. Mary sculpts, or dances, or sings. Sharon teaches and shares keen insights which challenge the minds of others. Frank offers hospitality. Betty eases hurts among the sad and the lonely. Each one brings something vital to the life of the community. Yet it matters greatly whether these gifts are merely noted in passing, or encouraged, supported, and praised. I have seen communities starve for lack of internal appreciation. I have seen them flourish when such appreciation is quietly given.

As community members, it can be helpful for us to

pause alone and prayerfully reflect on the gifts of others. What particular skill does this one bring? What special talent? What offering of insight or personality? Who is doing a job I would not dare to take on myself? We need to practice appreciation, considering carefully the gifts that others share and letting them know what their offering means to us all. Wherever this happens, a community increases in strength and upbuilds itself in love.

3. *Prayer for Sensitivity to the Needs of Others.* It is wholly natural to bring our own concerns to any gathering of our community. This is true even when we are meeting casually with just one or two others. Our personal hurts, our joys, our wonderings are bound to be in our minds. It is right that we find in community the place to share these matters. We are not meant to bury them or keep them tucked within.

Yet in one of the richest passages dealing with how the Christian community should model its own life on the life of Christ, the apostle Paul counsels us to be fully as sensitive to one another's needs as we are to our own (Phil 2:1-7). We may wish to pray for sensitivity before a time of gathering with others. We may even pray within while the period of togetherness proceeds. "Help me to listen, truly listen, to what this one is trying to say." "Open me to the needs that are here, Lord, that I may feel them within." "Guide me to respond in a way which will upbuild, even if all I do is listen and show that I have understood." Prayers for sensitivity can help us grow more receptive, and respond more lovingly, to the needs which arise in community life.

4. *The Discipline of Participation.* It is obvious that when people do not participate there is no community. It is equally obvious that when persons participate wholeheartedly community grows. As clear as these two matters may be, it is important to carry them in mind. Our participation in community is both joy and discipline. It is joy because of the richness and growth we find. It is

discipline because even where community life is strong we can drift, turn inward, or awaken to find that we are offering less than we truly can. If we wish to upbuild the spirit of love in our community, we need to check ourselves. We need to assess where we are. We prayerfully need to seek that our participation be full.

5. *Meditation on Biblical Images of the Church*. The New Testament pulses with brief images which depict the nature of Christian community. Jesus offered such images in his teachings. Paul employed them in his letters, as did the writers of the other epistles and the Apocalypse. At times the followers of Jesus are called *servants, the light of the world, the salt of the earth, saints, the people of God*. They are *flock, fruit, disciples, a fellowship, the body of Christ*. Empowered by the Spirit, they become *letters from Christ, messengers of reconciliation, a new humanity, the witnessing community*. And this by no means exhausts the list. On page after page of scripture, quick pictures flash forth. Each yields its own particular illumination.

Meditation on a biblical image of the church can deepen our understanding of Christian community. After selecting an image for meditation, begin with a time of coming to quiet. Pray for God's guidance during your reflections. Following this, simply focus on the image itself and rest in its presence. Then gently turn your considerations to all those places where you have seen this image lived out in the life of the church. Where have you seen a community which has truly become flock, or fruit, or the new humanity, or a light to the world? Call forth the instances from the past and from your own experience. Let your mind dwell on what you find there. Then once again move your thoughts gently, this time focusing on your own particular Christian community. Where has this image come to life in your community? Picture those moments, taking time to experience the reality of them anew. Finally, where can this image come to life in the future of your community? Let the scenes of possibility arise before you. In closing, give thanks for the image and the illumination that it spreads. Pray to keep the image before you and to reach for its realization in your life and in the life of your community.

6. Scriptural Examination of Community Life. At many points in scripture we find passages which can help communities join in evaluating certain aspects of their life together. In Matthew 5:21-26 Jesus offers words on reconciliation which certainly have applications within community life. In John 15:1-17 he calls on his followers to unite and bear fruit for him in the world. The qualities of love Paul points to in I Corinthians 13:4-7, the spiritual growth he prays for in Ephesians 3:14-19, and the practical gestures he cites in Romans 12:9-13 all touch directly on the life we share in Christian community. Scripture passages of this nature will provide a group with the basis for a thoughtful, prayerful examination of its own life.

The process of examination may begin with a reading of the passage and prayer for openness, both to God's word and to the words which will be shared within the group. After a time of quiet reflection on the scripture, members may be invited to speak of any places where they feel the community has been graced in its life. Where has the community mirrored the words of the scripture passage? Where have the counsels been kept? What positive directions are emerging? Then after this and a further time of quiet, all members can be invited to share where they feel the community is falling short of the words in the passage. Where has there been drifting or stumbling? Where does the community most need to grow?

The movement of such an examination is toward neither accusation nor self-congratulations. Its simple intent is to provide members with an opportunity to examine their common life in light of God's word and then to offer that life up once again in prayer. In view of this, it is fitting to close the time of self-examination with thanksgiving for those strengths the group has been given and petition that the group may grow stronger in the areas of its need.

7. Prayerful Approach to Tensions. This is not a tactic. It is not one more technique amid the already numerous helpful techniques for conflict resolution. The prayerful approach to tensions is, rather, the proper undergirding for all our words, our thoughts, our listening in any situation of interpersonal tension where we find ourselves. In Christian community, as in any other locus of human activity, such tension thrusts us into a variety of roles. At times it bursts upon us and we are the dumbfounded, the openmouthed, the shocked. "Where did all this come from?" we gasp. At times we are the recipients of gentle correction, and at times we must offer that correction. We are variously a front-line participant in tension, a mediator, a counselor, or the quiet witness to some problem which begs to be brought out into the open. Our roles change, as do the demands placed upon us in those roles. What remains constant, however, is the need to keep ourselves open through prayer in whatever role we may find ourselves.

For what we do we pray in situations of tension? Reconciliation and growth in understanding are obvious ends, but prayer for these matters alone may well leave us closed to what we really need to help us get there. Common experience points to additional prayer needs. For myself, and I am sure for many others, I find I am far better able to receive necessary words of correction from the person who has truly sought God's wisdom in what to say than from the person who speaks out of a barely controlled anger. And, what is really more important, whether or not that person approaches me with sensitivity, I am far better able to hear what I need to if I am inwardly praying to listen rather than trying to shore up my defenses. Similarly, I have witnessed mediators and counselors handle conflict with the greatest skill when their own inner preparations included prayer for wisdom and for sensitivity to all elements emerging in the situation.

For what then do we pray? In places of tension we need to pray steadily for those qualities of openness, sensitivity and receptivity which will further the process of reconciliation and growth. We need to pray for these qualities within ourselves as surely as we pray for them within others. We need to ask God's guidance for our speaking, our listening, our perceptions. When tensions arise unexpectedly, our prayers may be as swift as they are intense. They may come to no more than a single word or a sudden yearning of the mind and heart. We may continue in prayer for our openness during the whole time of our participation. If we perceive a tension in advance of its open expression then, whether we are to take the role of a counselor or a partisan, it is well to pray for God's special presence and working among all who will be drawn into the matter. And when a time of tension is past it is well to commit the situation, and the growth of all participants, to God's continuing care.

In short, the prayerful approach to tensions in Christian community is not a substitute for solid thought, honest speaking, and steady striving for a resolution. It is rather a gift by which all the thought, the speaking, and the striving can be thrown open to the One whose love and wisdom are infinitely vaster than our own. The prayerful approach to tensions may or may not hasten the process by which a resolution is found. It will, however, lift both the process and the participants to the plane of God's healing, growth-giving love.

8. *Thanksgiving for the Blessings of Community.* There are times when we simply need to pause and grow in gratitude for the blessings of our community. We need to examine our experience and give thanks for the specific elements of goodness that we find. What have we recently learned from another person's gifts? Or from a difficulty we are seeking to cope with? Or from a personality? Or from a moment of friendship and sharing? What new vision have

we gained about the extension of Christ's love in the world? Or about what we ourselves have to offer for him? Where is our community most stretching us in the ways of his love?

The blessings we find will vary from one time of our looking to the next. They may stand forth boldly from a celebration, lie hidden at the heart of a patience-wrenching experience, or extend quietly along the surface of a routine we have nearly taken for granted. As we pause to reflect and give thanks, our perspective grows. So does our sense of the ways Christ is at work among us. Most central, we are, with love, returning our gratitude for the Love which is being given.

Two Exercises

The Practice of Appreciation

1. Call to mind a member of your community on whom you wish to reflect. Ask for God's guidance as you consider this person.

2. Think on this person's gifts. What is he or she offering to your community? What abilities or traits of personality give richness? In what ways has this one been of special help to you? As you reflect you may wish to list the qualities and gifts that come to mind. You may want to focus for a time on images of that person actually sharing with others and with you.

3. Decide on some simple word you can speak or action you can take to let this other know of your appreciation.

4. Close your time of reflection by giving thanks to God for the place this other one holds in your community life and by asking that you may freely and sensitively express the gratitude you feel.

Scriptural Examination of Community Life
(Text: I Corinthians 13:4-7)

Structure: It will be helpful for all participants to have a bible, or at least a copy of the verses from I Corinthians. Let one member of the group serve as leader. Although this person's primary role is to draw forth the reflections of others, she or he should be free to offer perceptions too. From the start, participants should be helped to understand that the primary purpose of this exercise is not to reach firm, voted-upon conclusions. It is rather to elicit the present insights and concerns of the group and then to offer these in prayer.

1. The process can begin with the leader reading the passage and offering prayer for God's grace in this time of drawing together. In the prayer the leader may wish to include petition for freedom and honesty in sharing, for the willingness to listen, and for group discernment in coming to a richer sense of the community's strengths and needs.

2. The leader shall invite group members to reflect in silence on the passage. Where have the qualities of patience and kindness shown in community life? Where have there been the gifts of humility . . . hope . . . delight in the truth . . . trust? After the time of quiet consideration the leader shall encourage members to share their thoughts.

3. The leader shall again invite group members to reflect in silence on the passage, this time directing their thoughts toward the places of most needed growth. In what areas do community members feel the greatest need for God's grace in their community life right now? Where has the community drifted from the counsels of Paul? After further quiet reflection, the leader shall once again encourage group members to share their thoughts and concerns.

4. In closing, let the community join in a period of prayer. Members may be encouraged to offer thanks for the

specific blessings they are finding and prayers for God's grace in the areas of community need. The leader may read one last time the passage from scripture and offer a prayer of thanksgiving for God's presence in this occasion of sharing.

Scripture Passages

Additional passages for reading and meditation:

Psalm 133
Matthew 5:12-16
Matthew 5:21-26
Mark 4:26-32
Mark 10:28-31
Luke 17:20-21
John 1:9-13
John 15:1-17
Acts 2:42-47
Romans 12:1-13
I Corinthians 3:1-9
I Corinthians 8

I Corinthians 12
II Corinthians 3:1-6
II Corinthians 5:16-21
II Corinthians 8:1-7
Galatians 6:1-5
Ephesians 3:14-19
Ephesians 4:1-16
Ephesians 6:18-20
Philippians 4:2-3
Colossians 3:12-17
II Thessalonians 1:3-5
I Peter 2:9-10

A PRAYER
For the Community of the Christian Church

O Gracious God, we humbly pray for Your Holy Catholic Church, that You would be pleased to fill it with all truth in all peace. Where it is corrupt, purify it; where it is in error, direct it; where in any thing it is amiss, reform it. Where it is right, establish it; where it is in want, provide for it; where it is divided, reunite it. This we pray for the sake of Him who died and rose again and ever lives to make intercession for us, Jesus Christ Your Son our Lord.

Amen.

—**Adapted from** *The Book of Common Worship* **(The Presbyterian Church in the United States of America)**

7

God's World

God saw all he had made, and indeed it was very good.
—Genesis 1:31 (JB)

Ravaged, ravaged the earth,
despoiled, despoiled,
as Yahweh has said.
The earth is mourning, withering,
the world is pining, withering,
the heavens are pining away with the earth.
The earth is defiled
under its inhabitants' feet,
for they have transgressed the law,
violated the precept,
broken the everlasting covenant.
—Isaiah 24:3-5 (JB)

The poor and needy ask for water, and there is none,
their tongue is parched with thirst.
I, Yahweh, will answer them,
I, the God of Israel, will not abandon them.
—Isaiah 41:17 (JB)

The Landscape

A small greenish rock occupies a special place in our home. Some years ago skilled hands fashioned it into the shape of a duck. Or rather the hands managed to draw out the duck which was hiding in a chunk of soapstone which, in turn, had been drawn from an ancient and sacred outcropping of rock in California. The duck's neck curves gently backward. The head rests above the wings, pointing toward the tail. Waxy flecks of white in the rock suggest feathers. Near its breast, the duck's right wing curls just slightly under the body. Its eyes are closed.

The artist was a tall Native American named Dave Big Bear who lived in the St. Lawrence River Valley, not far from where my wife and I made our first home. When Dave cupped his muscular hands around the duck and brought it forth to show us, I couldn't help but notice a certain sadness in the way he cradled it and then set it slowly down on his workbench. He had obviously lavished great care on this particular carving. Was he regretful at the possibility of letting it go?

"Oh no, not really," he said softly. "It's just the circumstances." He went on to explain that some months before he had seen the photograph of a lone duck which had gotten trapped in the great dark smudge of an oil spill. The duck had died. "It was such a beautiful bird. I just had to do something."

When we left that day, Dave Big Bear wrapped the duck with extra care. We have cherished it ever since. In addition to being very beautiful, the sculpture is a memorial, a quiet cry.

Few incidents have so impressed me with the nature of the world we live in. This world, God's world, is a place of exquisite beauty. The beauty sometimes startles us, shakes us, and rattles us into realizing it is still here. We want to catch the beauty, cup it in our hands, hold it close. We do not want to lose it. Nevertheless, the world is also unquestionably a place of loss. The beauty is blasted, or covered over, or smudged, or hoarded by the few while the many must look on from afar. And it is also a world in which the sensitive and the responsible say, "I have to do something." It is these three distinct elements which mark the present landscape of God's world: beauty, loss, the need to respond.

The beauty sometimes shines in the simplest ways. A

child skips a stone into the chilled waters off the Maine coast and squints toward the sun as the stone hops three times before arching under a wall of foam. Gulls call overhead. Salt touches the child's lips. For a few moments the child stands stock still amid the roaring and the perpetual spray. Then, laughing aloud, she races back from the last dash of a spent wave, stops, cuts hard to the right and darts along the beach in search of another stone. In ten seconds the cycle of child and stone and waves begins again. If we are watching all this, we forget ourselves. If we are the child, we take it in and don't forget. With no words at all, the beauty has spoken.

I once knew a woman over 80 who lived near Chicago a few blocks back from the shore of Lake Michigan. Whenever she couldn't sleep she would get out of bed at four in the morning, bundle up, and haul the wooden chair from her kitchen onto the eastward-facing porch of her house. Other buildings cut off her view of the horizon, but she would sit there, utterly relaxed, waiting for the sun to come up. At length a soft gray, and sometimes pink, drifted above the neighboring buildings. If I ran into her any time during the following week, she would venture, "I saw the most wonderful sunrise." Half the time she would add in her aging voice, "It's still such a beautiful world."

The writers of the Book of Genesis gave a description of the beauty which pointed to something deeper than the beauty itself. The whole creation was "very good." Biblical scholar Gerhard von Rad notes that in the reserved language of the priestly writers this was tantamount to saying it was perfect. Chapters 1 and 2 of Genesis shine with images of overflowing abundance, intricate harmony, and the lush garden which is to be our home. Other books in the Bible continue to play upon these themes. Psalmists sing the glories of the nighttime sky and grain-ripened fields. The writers of Proverbs note a wisdom tucked into all creation from the very start. In the New Testament, when Paul and later John lift up scenes of diverse peoples living in peace, they do this in terms of the creation being restored. God created the world perfect, and when we catch our breath at a sunrise or take joy in the sight of children who do not know what it is to be prejudiced, we have, for a moment, glimpsed the lingering perfection.

Even a lingering perfection can lift our spirits. Nearly every day at noon I walk along a maple-covered bluff above the Clarion River in western Pennsylvania. In the summer I am surrounded by great, impenetrable pillows of green. In the winter I can gaze for miles over the gray, rolling hills that stretch beyond the river. At any season, when I return home I am renewed. Another person may, with great wisdom, treat all life as sacramental. Still another, in disciplined meditation, will reach toward the wisdom at the heart of creation. With giant accelerators and electron microscopes, another probes the tiniest known particles in the universe. Each in his or her own way is taking part in the endless exploration of mystery and wonder. Whether or not the vocabulary of Christian theology is used, each is in touch with the elemental perfection of all things that have been made.

Yet such moments of contact are fragmentary. Any thoughtful view of the world lets us know that the perfection we rejoice in is indeed a lingering perfection. The loss is real. Part of the refreshment that comes from seeing the goodness God created lies in the fact that our moments of seeing show us what appears to be so new, so fresh, so utterly different.

We hardly need recount once more the details of what has happened. We have heard the figures of imbalance in the world's goods to the point where we can almost recite them on our own. Abundance? The blessing persists, but where has the abundance flowed? Visions of all people living in peace are relentlessly fractured by dark-stained photographs of racial and political strife. The object of a day's destruction may be a duck, or a mountainside, or a child in Sri Lanka, or a miner in Appalachia. The tragedy, and that is not too strong a word, the tragedy is that each, at some point in the workings of the world, has become expendable. We hear the facts, the figures, the litany of loss. Here and there steps are taken: a stream is cleared, a crop sown, a truce signed, a moment of hard-won joy breaks out. But still the darker events continue. The gnawing reality of loss returns and takes hold once again.

At this point in our exploration of the landscape, we come directly upon two differing models of how we should conduct ourselves in God's world. One of these presents itself rather boldly as causing much of the loss. The other slides forth quietly as a temptation. These are, quite simply, the model of dominance and the model of romantic withdrawal. The model of dominance is easy to spot. It rests on a mistaken idea of what it means to have dominion over the beasts of the field and the birds of the air. It builds on the desire to accumulate all that one can for one's own kind, one's kindred, one's self. It expresses itself in exploitation of the earth and in the trampling of other people's rights. Its end results are use without restoration, gathering without distribution and, ultimately, destruction. The practice of dominance is relatively easy to denounce. To control it, however, is obviously a very different matter. Under its influence species and prairies continue to vanish, ancient water tables and whole peoples are bled dry.

Yet for me, and I suspect for many others of my bent, the model of romantic withdrawal is at least as difficult to counteract. I am tempted to walk forever along the bluffs of the Clarion River. Amid the losses in God's world, it is enticing just to immerse ourselves in the places of beauty that remain. Enjoy. Forget the rest. Hold on to the best as long as you can. . . "As long as you can. . ." I consider, and I start to realize that if all I do is walk the bluffs, I shall do so only until one day, perhaps ages and ages hence, dominance seizes the bluffs, scours them, and scrubs them flat. If all I do is gaze after the subatomic wonders of the lepton and the quark, I shall be able to do so only until some awesome blast on the atomic level forever melts any minds that might have found joy in these fleeting bits of perfection. By itself immersion in the beauty that remains is not enough. Romantic withdrawal is a very dead end. It puts us to sleep while dominance advances and takes control. Enjoy the beauty, yes. We need it. It renews us. It reminds us of a deep goodness we too easily forget. But, also, we need to remember the loss. It is only when we remember the loss in God's world that we sense deep within the need to respond.

The scriptures offer us a very different model of our role in creation. This model takes with full seriousness our need to respond to the loss. It sets us against the ravages brought by dominance and allowed by romantic withdrawal. Our role is, quite simply, that of the caretaker. From the start we have been placed in the garden to till it and keep it. We are God's representatives, God's stewards. We are not to live off the garden until it lies brown and exhausted, nor are we here for a perpetual vacation. We are to tend the greenness, nourish the abundance, care for the balance. In a fallen world this takes the sweat of our brow and the toil of our minds and hands. It is not a one-time effort. It is a continuous job, age in age out.

Our role as caretaker is undergirded by other powerful themes in scripture. On whatever level we interpret the story of Noah, it is clear from God's covenant at the end that "never again" will God act to destroy the earth. God is on the side of preservation. If destruction comes, it will be from our own hand. In the Magnificat, we find the culmination of what prophets foretold for centuries:

> He has shown the power of his arm,
> he has routed the proud of heart.
> He has pulled down princes from their thrones
>   and exalted the lowly.
> The hungry he has filled with good things,
>   the rich sent empty away (Lk 1:51-53, *JB*).

In Christ, God acts to restore the balance of a broken world. What has been hoarded shall, in his name, be shared by all. Paul rightly sees that this restoration arches out to tear down ancient barriers of hostility and create a single people in place of the world's warring factions. As caretakers we are not alone. Even our feeblest deeds are supported by the unremitting will and actions of the loving God.

In God's world, then, our love is an active love. It needs to take root through periods of nourishment within our own lives. With our walks, our wonder, our days of recreation we can glimpse afresh the goodness God has made. With our minds and hearts we can probe images of the perfection God intends. Such times deepen our love even as they rekindle our spirits. Beyond any of this, however, our love must act. Whether we plant, or sculpt, or write, or engage in political action, we must bend the talents God has given us to the task at hand. To love God's world is to labor for a restoration of the fellowship of humankind and to give ourselves to renewing the vibrant freshness of the earth.

Approaches

As we seek to grow in our love for God's world we need to deepen our own appreciation for the goodness God has made. We need to grasp the beauty and hold it close within. At the same time, we need to strengthen our resolve and our action as caretakers in the world. The inward deepening and the outward deeds go together. In the following suggestions the first three focus on the nourishment of our inner appreciation and sensitivity. The remaining five carry us from inner growth to action on a variety of levels.

1. *Walking and Receiving*. We can walk just for the exercise. We can walk to get from our office to our car, from the barn to the house, from the apartment to the library. We go from point A to point B and are thankful for the stretch of our muscles or, perhaps, are thankful that we wound up

where we intended. When it comes to walking and growing in our love for God's world, however, it is not the destination that matters most. It is not even the exercise. What matters most is simply the receiving. For our growth within, walking and receiving go hand in hand.

Many persons find it helpful to follow nearly the same path every day. The very sameness lets us forget about what our feet are doing and receive of the steady goodness and the surprises that are taking place around us. I like to imagine that near where I grew up an eight-block stretch of sidewalk bears the microscopic indentation eroded there by my father as he made his daily walk in his later years. He returned from these ventures with ever-fresh gifts. One day it was the sight of a bud. The next day, "Lake Michigan is the bluest it's been in years." The next day it was tales of a six-year-old boy who popped out from nowhere and plied him with every question under the sun.

We cannot dictate what the gifts from a day's walk shall be. We can only take ourselves and our openness. If we do this, though, the goodness still lying at the heart of God's creation shall reach out and touch us. As pure grace, it shall increase the joy and wonder that we know within.

2. Immersion in the Goodness. Our experience of the goodness in God's world is not limited to those occasions when we go forth physically. Just while sitting still we can take time to immerse ourselves in the beauty that has been made. We can close our eyes, and then select an image. It may be something as immediate as a flower or as vast as the black and silver dome of a star-studded sky. It may be as vital as a scene of different races living in the harmony God intended. We need to let the image rise before us and then gradually we can enter into its fullness. Sense the freshness. Probe the intimacy. Perceive the wisdom lying at the very heart of what we view. Allow ourselves to grow in gratitude for the goodness we are finding. As our time of meditation draws to a close, we can offer thanksgiving and also our prayers to remain sensitive to the beauty God has intended for all creation.

3. *Cultivating Our Sensitivity*. Sensitivity often appears to be purely a gift. An artist sees colors which the rest of us miss. A skilled counselor hears healing insights tucked away in hurried remarks. A person devoted to some particular social reform is gripped by needs which the rest of society has not yet discovered. If we call such people "gifted," we are right. Their sensitivity outreaches our own. They inform and challenge us with what they find.

Yet among persons of gifted sensitivity, we repeatedly see two traits from which the rest of us can learn: such persons know how to pause; they know how to reflect. These are the inner disciplines which can nourish the sensitivities God has given us all. We need to learn to pause frequently over what we encounter in the world. It may be the sound of laughter in our neighborhood that arrests us, or a cry of pain. It may be the sight of a toddler racing toward a pair of outstretched arms. We may be caught by some image of inhumanity, or a breath of hope, on the evening news. Our reflections at such times will often be brief, but even brief reflections can heighten our awareness. How do we feel about what we have just encountered? What images does it press on our mind? What details of beauty or hurt do we wish to remember? Pause . . . reflect. Let these two elements become a daily part of even our casual movements in the world. As they are transformed into a gentle habit, our sensitivity will grow.

4. *Meditation/Action on God's Provision for Our Needs*. This exercise and the three which come after it all involve a time of meditation which is then followed by actions growing out of the meditation.

For this particular exercise, after a time of coming to quiet and prayer for God's guidance in your meditation, call forth the various ways God has provided for you in your life. Dwell first on the provisions God has made for your body.

Consider food . . . clothing . . . shelter. You may wish to let your mind rest in the presence of these provisions. Then consider the provisions God has made for your spirit: friendships . . . enjoyments and places of rest . . . gifts of word and sacrament and Spirit. Let yourself grow in gratitude for all that God has shared.

Still in meditation, move now to a time of evaluation. Of all the provisions God has made, are there any specific ones which you have cheapened through misuse? Forgotten? Taken for granted? Are there any which you have used too much? Are there any which you ought to share with others more than you have been doing? As you proceed with your evaluation, write down the thoughts that come to you.

Closing your meditation and moving toward action, look over the list you have just made. Select those two or three insights on which you most need to act. Prayerfully determine the step or steps you will take. Write these down as an act of commitment. Ask God to sustain you in your commitment, and return thanks once again for the abundance of God's provisions in your life. In a period of not more than three weeks, it will be well to evaluate prayerfully the steps you have taken, to pray for new light where you need it, and to offer thanks for God's continuing care.

5. Meditation/Action on the Places of Hurt. Begin with a time of prayer for God's guidance, both in growing sensitive to the hurts in the world around you and in finding ways to respond that will be in the spirit of Christ. Then, in quietness, let images of the world's hurts and injustices come into your mind. These may be very personal images, sharply focused: a hungry child, a victim of domestic violence, a ruined hillside, an unemployed worker. Your mind may lay hold on more sweeping images: the imbalance of wealth among the nations of the earth, the preparations for war and neglect of human needs, whole peoples deprived of their rights, the ruin of natural resources which are needed both for their beauty and for sustaining the populations of the earth. Let the images of hurt come to you. Dwell on them for a time. Write them down.

From the list you have made, select the hurt to which you feel you can most effectively respond. Prayerfully consider each of the following: 1) What can you personally say that will help others grow aware of this hurt? 2) What can you do in your own life-style or personal actions which will in some way respond to this hurt? 3) What actions can you urge on the public level which will help treat this hurt? Write down your responses as a personal commitment.

Close your time of meditation asking that you remain sensitive to all the places of hurt you encounter. Ask for wisdom and perseverance in following through on the commitments you have made. As you move into the time of fulfilling those commitments, continue to seek new insights, both into the hurt and into the responses that can be made.

6. Meditation/Action on Our Role as Caretaker. Begin this exercise by imagining yourself as one of a large number of persons in the midst of an immense garden. Take time to acquaint yourself with the garden. Picture all the beautiful things that are there, the sights, the abundance of goods, the freshness of life, the concord among some of its inhabitants. Dwell on the positive images you find. Then take time to acquaint yourself with those places where the garden has been abused. What signs of neglect do you see? Of destruction? Of discord among its inhabitants? Be present to these negative images and feel the loss they indicate.

Now imagine some of the inhabitants working as caretakers in the garden. Follow these persons in your mind as they go about their different tasks. What are some of them doing to maintain the places of beauty? What are others doing to restore harmony and build up the wasteland? You may wish to write down the responses that you see.

Lastly, view yourself as among those who are caretakers of the garden. What do you do? What are your specific lines of activity? List the things you see yourself doing to take care of the garden, and close with a prayer that you may remain responsible to your role as caretaker in all that you do.

7. *Meditation/Action: The Human Community*. A more detailed treatment of this approach appears in the second of the two exercises offered in the next section of this chapter. The process involves a time of focusing on images of the human community as God created it to be and then on images of division, strife, prejudice. After a period of self-examination and reflection on those places where God's intention for the human community is being restored, commitments are made to action in both the inner sphere of one's own attitudes and the outward arena of public acts.

8. *The Practice of Simplicity*. From the very start, the Lord of the church has said to his followers:

> "Fear not, little flock, for it is your Father's good pleasure to give you the kingdom. Sell your possessions and give alms; provide yourselves with purses that do not grow old" (Lk 12:32-33, *RSV*).

It is clear that there is no one set pattern for following this mandate. Some take vows of poverty and enter formal religious orders. Some families seek to follow the Lord's counsel of simplicity in what they accumulate and what they give. Some movements, such as the Puritans, the Quakers, the Church of the Brethren, give striking witness to the call for simplicity through their own evolving practices. Simplicity comes forth in a variety of personal and community forms. It is clear too, though, that wherever persons follow the counsel of simplicity they are set free to grow in their sense of the limitless abundance God provides. Whatever movement they may be a part of, whatever path of simplicity they may take, such persons are liberated for generosity and bold acts of caring in the world.

The practice of simplicity is exactly that: a practice. What am I seeking in life, or protecting, that I really don't need? No matter how far we have moved in the direction of simplicity, the question always has new answers. Where can I grow in my reliance on God's provision for my life? What new offerings can I make of material goods, and of myself, to help treat the hurts and preserve the beauties of the world? It is as we develop the habit of such questions that our perceptions grow. It is as we act on these perceptions that, with God's aid, we move into the truly free and creative life God has called us to.

Two Exercises

Immersion in the Goodness

1. Take time to relax completely, closing your eyes until all sense of tension is gone.

2. As you continue in quietness, call forth a single image of something that is particularly beautiful to you. It may be a tree, a flower, or a cluster of stars. It may be a river, or the face of a friend, or a gesture of kindness. Let your mind rest for a time on that single image, gathering all the details of sight and touch and sound that you can.

3. Now enter more fully upon the object of your thoughts. View it from different angles. Sense its freshness . . . its intricacy . . . its depth of beauty and goodness. Allow yourself to grow in gratitude for what you are finding, pausing over details, images, insights.

4. Return gently to the image with which you began. Offer thanksgiving for the beauty you have seen and pray that you may remain sensitive to all the goodness God has made.

Meditation/Action: The Human Community

1. After a time of quieting and prayer for God's illumination, call to mind images of the human community as God created it to be. Let these images be as

particular and specific or as broad and sweeping as is natural for you. They may include scenes such as racial harmony, or peace among nations, or people sharing and all having enough. Take time to rest in the presence of the images that come to you and to give thanks for them.

2. Turn your mind now to images of breakdown and hurt in the human community. Again let arise within you such images as are natural for you: recent scenes from world events, or difficult personal experiences, or deeds of prejudice and oppression that you have heard of. Take time to dwell in the presence of these harsh realities, sensing the hurt and the loss they bring.

3. Turn within yourself now for a period of prayerful self-examination. Asking God's guidance, seek out any places of prejudice or hostility in your own life . . . any groups you treat with little patience . . . or with no hope. Where do you greet hurts in the human community with indifference? Where do you need to grow in your knowledge of what is happening, in your openness to what God is trying to say? As a source of guidance and a commitment to act, write down any insights that come to you during this time.

4. Move now to focus on outward acts of healing in the human community. Let come into your mind images of persons working to end warfare, to feed the hungry and redress the imbalance of rich and poor, or to end the spirit of prejudice, or to bring wholeness of life to the oppressed. Then consider: Where have you been privileged to take part in such healing works, even if your part seemed to be just a small one? In what ways can you give yourself now to the healing of the human family? As a commitment to continue and to grow, write down your responses.

5. In closing, look over the commitments you have listed for both inward and outward growth as a healer in the human community. Give thanks for the insights you have received. Pray for grace to follow them. Set yourself a time when you will come back again, review where you are, and seek continuing grace and guidance.

Scripture Passages

Additional passages appropriate for reading and meditation:

Genesis 1:1 — 2:3
Genesis 2:15-25
Genesis 9:8-17
Leviticus 25:23
Psalms 8, 19:1-6, 24:1-2
    33:1-9, 65:9-13, 104,
    136:1-9, 148
Proverbs 3:19-20
Proverbs 8:22-31
Isaiah 5:8-10
Isaiah 11:1-9

Isaiah 35
Jeremiah 2:7
Matthew 6:25-33
Luke 1:46-55
John 1:1-3
Ephesians 1:9-10
Ephesians 2:11-22
Colossians 3:11
I Timothy 4:1-5
Revelation 21:1-4
Revelation 22:1-4

A PRAYER
To Act for the Restoration of God's World

Lord, strengthen us in these troublous times. Save us from a retreat into hatred or despair. Call us out of the shelters and send us up to the roofs, even if day and night we are under fire. Help us to rebuild the house that is broken down, and to put out the flames before they destroy us all. Rebuke us for any self-pity, and teach us rather to keep our pity for others who need it. May we remain calm in the midst of violence and panic, and may reason and love and mercy and understanding rule our lives. And may we this coming day be able to do some work of peace for Thee.

—**Alan Paton** in *Instrument of Thy Peace* (**Seabury Press, 1968**)

Epilogue: Glimpses

As a small boy I thought it would be great fun to have a vision. When I was six I went to a movie in which an old holy man in India had a vision just before he died. He was out in the middle of a wasteland when all of a sudden the yellowed ground turned green, the dry river bed gushed with water, and the copper sky was transformed into the richest blue. He stepped into the midst of all this and, after the Hollywood dialogue patterns of the time, said something like, "This is it!" Then the whole scene faded — the blue sky, the flowing waters, the green fields, the old man and all. I went out of the theater saying, in my child's mind, "That was neat!" As a rare dispensation, I got to see the movie a second time.

Well, I am middle-aged now and have yet to see a vision. I have, though, caught glimpses. And these glimpses have really had nothing to do with the application of special effects, celluloid overlays, or even the flights of creative imagination. They are rock solid, utterly real, flesh and blood, passing before my eyes in some surprise moment of a day or evening. To say the very least, when I pause to think on these glimpses they bring me fully as much joy as ever did that particular event I saw on the screen so many years ago.

The glimpses, I should hurry to add, are not one in kind with those special visions which I do believe have been granted from the days of the prophets onward as a gift to rare individuals. My glimpses are earthy and neighborhood bound. They catch within their scope one friend here or another over there. They sometimes focus on two or three working together, or on a whole body of people clustered around a common task. In sum, my glimpses are of persons who have heard the call to love and, in a myriad of ways, are seeking to respond.

There are times when the glimpses are exactly that, glimpses, and nothing more. They come as a sudden flash, a onetime viewing of strangers, a peek into the best that others have to give. In an emergency room many miles from our home I watch as a doctor shares agonizing words with an older woman from one of my parishes. He is young, but has already worked at this most difficult part of his job and is wise enough not to hide his own pain as he speaks. Even as his words cut and slice, his compassion heals, as much as anything can heal in those moments. Neither the woman nor I shall ever see that doctor again. But we won't forget him either, and the memory of him will forever be present as a warmth amid the sorrow of what he had to share. Or on a lighter plane, the third cross-country bike camp of the summer unpacks its gear for a one-night stand in our church basement. I watch anxiously. Will they be like the last group we had, which nearly cost us our janitor? Or will they be like the first group, which was nice and tidy? In short order, I come to see they will be like neither. Tidiness isn't the issue. They have two splendid counselors and, amid all the natural aches of cycling, 15 young people have come alive with the desire to support one another. When they head on their way the next morning I am refreshed not by their departure but by the spirit that they leave behind.

At times the glimpses appear in serial fashion. They run backward, as it were, through an extended period of time. In a tense meeting I watch as a friend struggles to overcome a prejudice that has limited her love and the love of her neighbors for years. As she speaks my mind's eye catches images of her at wholly different moments in her life. I see her when she helped three young children cope with the trauma of a sudden divorce, and when night after night she checked on the needs of an elderly man next door, and when she poured every ounce of her awesome enthusiasm into bringing joy to a kids' volleyball team. "*Great*, you made it!" or "*Great*, you did your best!" My images of her break off at the point where I first met her, but I know the outreachings of love were there long before I viewed them.

Or I watch as a gathering of 30 persons in a parish commit themselves to minister over the next three months to needs that lie on their doorstep. Some will visit in the county jail. Two will give their time to young people who are facing difficult decisions. Others will call on the elderly, start a pre-school experience, help develop a medicine delivery system for the homebound. It is a rich night for that small religious community. Everything they commit themselves to comes to pass. As I watch them that night, though, my mind moves back to other moments when I have seen them in the years before. I see them gather to give support in times of mutual pain. I see them struggle to speak honestly and to understand one another in the face of a war that split the nation and divided them as well. I catch sight of them coming to my door during a season of family illness. I watch them celebrate with deep joy the births, the weddings, the anniversaries of community life. A single glimpse comes and others, stretching back through time, follow in its wake.

Sometimes the glimpses are purely personal. I look within myself and suddenly see that by the grace of God a hostility I have lugged about for ages is now giving way to something fresher and more understanding. I shall have to continue working at it, but the change is coming. Or I set out to respond to a pastoral need when too exhausted or too self-concerned to be of any use at all. When I return home I am enlivened, enriched, having been both stretched and graciously aided in what I was sure I could not do.

I can never conjure up a glimpse, nor can anybody else I know. Glimpses come ever as a gift. They are the sudden breakthroughs of love. They are as fresh, as joy giving, and as much of a perennial surprise as the first buds of spring. Yet in their uncontrollable multitude of forms, the glimpses flow together to remind me that the call to love is unending and the aid we need in responding comes without limit. Love itself will never run out of places to happen, and those who work to overcome a prejudice, or yearn to increase in devotion, or join in common effort to ease the hurts of others, will find God's steady, gracious aid for the growth they need.

In all of this I find a quiet comfort. For myself, I do not know what tomorrow will bring. I have my hunches and my hopes, but nothing more. It is the same for the day after that and the seasons after that. It is really the same for us all. The specifics of the future lie beyond our sight. But this much we do know, that in even the hardest events an opportunity to love will be there. So will the aid we need for growth in our loving. And wherever love is brought to life the barren ground shall indeed grow green, parched places be watered, and copper skies begin to turn the richest blue.

Appendix I
Suggestions for Study Groups and Retreats

For Study Groups — The book may be used in a series of eight meetings, or more if participants wish. Ideally the time allotted for each meeting will be in the neighborhood of an hour to an hour and a half. Movements of the meetings may be as follows:

The first meeting — Participants shall be encouraged to read chapter 1 in advance. During the meeting, in addition to discussing the main sections of the chapter, the leader can invite participants to reflect within themselves and then share with one another their responses to the following questions:

- What persons have they known in their own lives who have lived well the life of love?
- What spiritual practices have been the most aid to them over the years?
- As they look over the titles of the chapters in the book, where do they feel God is most calling them to grow in their ability to love?

For subsequent meetings — The group will focus on a different chapter at each meeting with participants reading the chapter during the week before. The meetings may each have three basic movements.

1. *Focus on the Landscape.* After drawing forth the main points made in the Landscape section of the chapter,

the leader can encourage the group to share its own further reflections. What do group members most identify with here? What would they want to underline as being important for themselves as individuals? for the group? for the Christian church today? Do they have other points and perspectives which they wish to add?

2. *Directed Meditation.* The leader may take the group through one of the exercises included in the chapter. After the time of meditation is over, the leader can encourage group members to share their experiences as fully as they wish to. It will be helpful if the leader notes that no two persons will have had exactly the same experience and that they will be able to learn from each other as they share.

3. *Approaches.* Allow time to look over and discuss the Approaches section of the chapter, and then let each participant select an approach to act on during the coming week. Time may be allowed at the start of the next meeting for participants to share their experiences and reflections if they wish.

The final meeting — Members shall read the Epilogue in advance. Discussion can move through a variety of summary questions and sharings in the group. Where have members of the group caught their own "glimpses" over the years? Where have they caught glimpses within the group itself? Looking back over the various focal points of the past weeks, where has God most aided them in this study? Where is God most calling them to grow in love right now?

On devotions — For devotions at the beginning or end of a group meeting it may be helpful to use a scripture from the list found at the end of each chapter and to have the group share in offering the prayer which concludes the chapter.

For Retreats — Here follows the outline for a 48-hour retreat on Growth in the Ways of Love. This format encourages participants to review within themselves, and together,

the full range of areas suggested in this book. Retreat planners may wish to narrow the focus, allowing more time for silence and personal reflection, or adapting to the amount of time available. *Presentations* may utilize materials from the chapters or sections indicated in parentheses. *Directed Meditations* may be drawn from the exercises relating to the materials under consideration. *Small Group Meetings* will allow participants to gather in groups of not more than eight to discuss with leaders and themselves their reflections on the presentation, to share their experiences with the directed meditation, and to receive and reflect on the list of Approaches relating to the topic of discussion.

Friday afternoon
   4:00   Arrival, getting settled
   5:00   Informal reception, time for getting acquainted
   6:00   Dinner

Friday evening
   7:00   Opening Presentation: *The Call and the Struggle* (chapter 1)
   7:45   Break
   8:00   Presentation: *God's Love for Us* (Landscape, chapter 2)
   8:30   Directed Meditation (from one of the Two Exercises, chapter 2): When the meditation is completed, participants may be encouraged to continue in silence or to move about as they wish until the time of the small group meetings.
   9:00   Small Group Meetings—A time for sharing introductions with one another; reflections on the presentation and on experiences of the meditation; distribution and discussion of Approaches list from chapter 2
  10:00   Evening Prayer, entire community gathered

Saturday morning
   7:30   Morning prayer
   8:00   Breakfast and time for personal reflection
   9:00   Presentation: *Our Love for God* (Landscape, chapter 3)
   9:30   Directed Meditation (chapter 3)
  10:00   Small Group Meetings — Reflections on the presentation, experiences of the meditation, distribution and discussion of Approaches list from chapter 3.
  10:45   Rest, personal prayer, reflection, walking
  11:30   Liturgy
  12:15   Lunch
Saturday afternoon
   1:30   Presentation: *My Neighbor* (Landscape, chapter 4)
   2:00   Directed Meditation (chapter 4)
   2:30   Small Groups — using previous format
   3:15   Rest, personal prayer, reflection, walking
   4:00   Presentation: *My Enemy* (Landscape, chapter 5)
   4:30   Directed Meditation (chapter 5)
   5:00   Small Groups
   5:45   Rest, personal prayer, and reflection
   6:30   Dinner
Saturday evening
   7:30   Presentation: *My Community* (Landscape, chapter 6)
   8:00   Directed Meditation (chapter 6)
   8:30   Small Groups
   9:30   Vesper Service
It may be helpful at this point in the weekend if the leaders are available for individual consultation, direction, and prayer.

Sunday morning
  7:30 Morning prayer
  8:00 Breakfast and time for personal reflection
  9:00 Presentation: *God's World* (Landscape, chapter 7)
  9:30 Directed Meditation (chapter 7)
  10:00 Small Groups
  10:45 Personal preparations for the liturgy
  11:00 Eucharistic Service
  12:15 Dinner
Sunday afternoon
  1:30 Brief Presentation: *An Invitation to Reflect —*
         Where is God calling us to grow?
  1:45 A time for personal reflections, planning, prayer
  2:30 Closing liturgy

Appendix II
Annotated Bibliography of Additional Readings

Contemporary and Current Works

Barth, Karl. "The Holy Spirit and the Upbuilding of the Christian Community" in *Church Dogmatics*, vol. IV-2, pp. 614-726; Edinburgh, T. & T. Clark, 1958. (Treats the nature, upbuilding, and continuance of Christian community.)

Bonhoeffer, Dietrich. *Life Together*; New York, NY: Harper & Row, 1954. (An exploration of the rhythms and sustaining bonds of Christian fellowship.)

Green, Thomas H., S.J. *Opening to God*; Notre Dame, IN: Ave Maria Press, 1977. (A helpful introduction to both the nature and the techniques of prayer.)

Hall, Douglas John. *The Steward—Biblical Symbol Come of Age*; New York, NY: Friendship Press, 1984. (Opening chapters explore the nature of our position as stewards of God's creation; chapters 6, 7 and 8 probe the implications of our role in relation to the global issues of environment, poverty, and political division.)

Lucien, Joseph Richard. *The Spirituality of John Calvin*; Atlanta, GA: John Knox Press, 1974. (A sensitive treatment of the common roots and differing emphases of Reformed and Roman Catholic spirituality.)

Minear, Paul S. *Images of the Church in the New Testament*; Philadelphia, PA: Westminster Press, 1960. (A helpful study of the early church's understanding of itself, written with particular sensitivity to the emerging ecumenical movement.)

Nouwen, Henri J.M. *With Open Hands*; Notre Dame, IN: Ave Maria Press, 1972. (Enriched by the photography of Ron P. Van Den Bosch and Theo Robert, the book probes the attitudes and movements of a maturing spirituality.)

Paton, Alan. *Instrument of Thy Peace*; New York, NY: Seabury Press, 1968. (In a series of meditations, Paton treats the intimate relation between the Prayer of St. Francis and the tasks facing Christians in the closing decades of the 20th century.)

Pennington, M. Basil, O.C.S.O. *Centering Prayer*; Garden City, NY: Doubleday & Co., 1980. (Provides an excellent history of the development of Eastern Christian spirituality as well as an extremely helpful presentation of a contemporary prayer practice.)

Classic Works

(*A happy reader's reflection*: Any classic must be read in a spirit of relaxation. The person who reads the opening chapters of *Moby Dick* and does not chuckle at least six times has brought too much awe to the task. The person who says of St. John of the Cross, "I can't make heads or tails of him!" is making poor St. John more difficult than anyone in the 16th century ever dreamed possible. If we read gently, and let the thought patterns of the writers become our own, their words will speak to our lives with the clarity and depth they have always possessed.)

Anonymous. *The Cloud of Unknowing and the Book of Privy Counseling*, ed. W. Johnston. Garden City, NY: Doubleday & Co., 1973.

Bunyan, John. *The Pilgrim's Progress*. Available in numerous editions.

Calvin, John. *Preface to the Commentaries on the Book of Psalms* in *Calvin's Commentaries*, trans. John King. Grand Rapids, MI: Wm. B. Eerdmans, 1972.

Luther, Martin. *A Simple Way to Pray*, reprinted in *Minister's Prayer Book*, ed. John W. Doberstein. Philadelphia, PA: Fortress Press, 1959. Recently reprinted by publisher.

St. John of the Cross. *Ascent of Mt. Carmel*, ed. E. Allison Peers. Garden City, NY: Doubleday & Co., 1958.

_____. *Dark Night of the Soul*, ed. E. Allison Peers. Garden City, NY: Doubleday & Co., 1959.

St. Ignatius Loyola. *The Spiritual Exercises of St. Ignatius*, trans. Louis J. Puhl, S.J. Chicago, IL: Loyola University Press, 1951.

_____. Also an extremely helpful reading of the *Exercises* is found in David L. Fleming, S.J. *Modern Spiritual Exercises—A Contemporary Reading of the Spiritual Exercises of St. Ignatius*. Garden City, NY: Doubleday & Co., 1978.